The Complete Photo Guide To

Paper Crafts

Creative Publishing international

Copyright © 2009 Creative Publishing international, Inc.
400 First Avenue North Suite 300
Minneapolis, Minnesota 55401
1-800-328-3895
www.creativepub.com

Printed in China

10 9 8 7 6 5 4 3 2 1

Library of Congress Cataloging-in-Publication Data

Boerens, Trice.
  The complete photo guide to paper crafts / Trice Boerens.
     p. cm.
  Includes index.
  Summary: "Techniques and projects in step-by-step format
for all kinds of paper crafts"–Provided by publisher.
  ISBN-13: 978-1-58923-528-1 (soft cover)
  ISBN-10: 1-58923-468-5 (soft cover)
  1. Paper work. I. Title.

TT870.B585 2010
745.54–dc22

2009024170

President/CEO: Ken Fund
Vice President/Sales & Marketing: Kevin Hamric
Publisher: Winnie Prentiss
Acquisition Editors: Linda Neubauer, Deborah Cannarella
Production Managers: Laura Hokkanen, Linda Halls
Creative Director: Michele Lanci-Altomare
Senior Design Managers: Jon Simpson, Brad Springer
Lead Photographer: Joel Schnell
Photographers: Corean Komarec, Kevin Dilley
Photo Coordinator: Joanne Wawra
Cover & Book Design: Val Escher
Page Layout: Val Escher
Copy Editor: Catherine Broberg

Visit www.Craftside.Typepad.com for a behind-the-scenes
peek at our crafty world!

Trice Boerens is an author of paper crafting, quilting,
jewelry making, and stitching books. She has also
worked as an art director, a magazine editor, and
a product packager. Living and working in the
foothills of the Wasatch Mountains in Ogden, Utah,
she is always on the lookout for new techniques and
unexpected inspiration.

The Complete Photo Guide To
Paper Crafts

cutting • folding • weaving • quilling • punching • collage • casting • journals • more

Creative Publishing
international

CONTENTS

Introduction

Hands down, the most common material used by artists and crafters worldwide is paper. It is familiar, user-friendly, and inexpensive. Paper can be cut, coiled, punched, glued, blended, molded, layered, folded, sculpted, and stitched.

Papers

Strolling through the paper aisles at a craft supply store or specialty paper craft store will reveal overwhelming choices of papers with solid colors and printed designs. Paper comes in a wide variety of weights and textures, too, which is an added enticement to paper crafters.

Mulberry paper is made from the bark of mulberry trees. Lightweight and organic in appearance, embedded strands of fiber make it strong enough to stretch and mold. It is favored by card makers for its beautiful feathered edge and is available in a rainbow of colors. Look for mulberry paper in craft and art supply stores.

Vellum, also available in craft and art supply stores, is a brittle, semi-transparent paper with a satin finish. Its polished surface and crisp cut edge lend it to formal applications such as wedding invitations. Use care when adhering it to any paper substrate. Vellum is not porous and therefore adhesives which are applied to the reverse side will show on the finished side. It is best to use small inconspicuous squares of double-sided adhesive.

Cardstock, sometimes referred to as cover stock, is the same weight as business cards and greeting cards.

Most porous papers have a grain or a north/south orientation. During the manufacturing process, the tiny cellulose fibers of the paper pulp are aligned parallel to each other. To achieve a smooth folded edge, bend with the grain of the paper.

Before folding medium- to heavyweight paper, score it by running a dull knife along the edge of a metal ruler. This creates an indentation that determines the fold line.

Cutting tools

Paper will dull the blades of your scissors. If you are working with fabric and paper, use two pairs of scissors and dedicate one pair to fabric, and one to paper. To sharpen your paper scissors, cut through fine sandpaper several times.

Paper will also dull the blades of your craft knife, and trimming with a dull blade will result in ragged edges. To achieve clean edges, change your blades often. Protect your craft table when using a craft knife by using a self-healing cutting mat. Use a metal edge ruler as a cutting guide and hold it firmly as you pass the knife along the edge. When cutting heavy paper, don't attempt to cut with one pass and heavy pressure. Instead, make several light passes with the knife.

Adhesives

If you are making heirloom scrapbook pages, use adhesives that will not discolor the paper or cause it to become brittle or to disintegrate. Products that are labeled as being archival will not damage your paper or your photos. Archival adhesives are available in tape or spray form.

Using spray adhesive to attach paper to paper is fast and convenient. Be careful to cover craft tables with newspaper before spraying the adhesive because the spray covers a wide area.

There are many projects that require double-sided adhesive. This product is available in sheet or tape form and is recommended for areas that require a tight grip. Cutting tape is faster than cutting sheets, but sheets can be trimmed to any shape or configuration. The adhesive will stick to your scissors, and will quickly build up along the blades. Clean your scissors often with steel wool or use scissors that are coated with a nonstick surface.

ADHESIVES FOR PAPER CRAFTS

Adhesive	Uses
spray adhesive	for large shapes of lightweight paper
rubber cement	for large shapes and those used to block out and define backgrounds
double-sided adhesive	for medium- to heavyweight papers
glue dots	for irregular shapes and accents

SURFACE DECORATION

There are many ways to texturize, color, or alter the appearance of paper to give it unique characteristics for whatever purpose you have in mind. With acrylic craft paints, watercolor paints, colored pencils, or chalks, you can use many of the same decorative techniques you would use for other craft materials. Try these ideas or experiment with other decorative techniques.

Techniques

MIRROR IMAGE

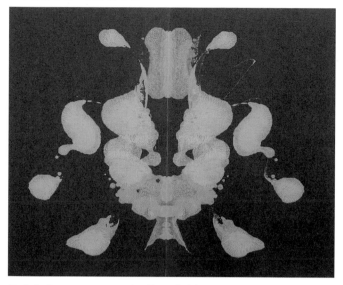

Fold the paper in half; unfold. Drop acrylic paint on one side; then refold and press the layers together.

BAS RELIEF

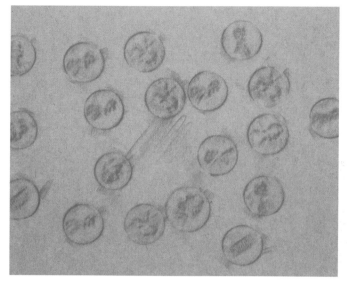

Place 3-D objects on the craft table. Place the paper on top and rub the flat side of a colored pencil over the surface.

POINTILLISM

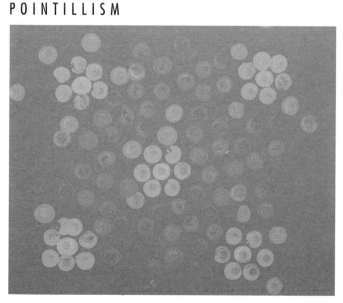

Dip the end of a pencil in a shallow pool of acrylic paint, and touch the tip to the paper.

MELTED WAX

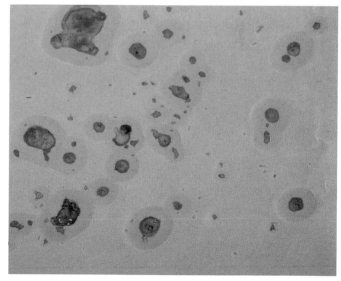

Shave bits of crayon onto the paper. Place between sheets of scrap paper and press with a hot iron. Apply a thin wash of diluted acrylic paint.

BATIK

Draw on medium-weight paper with crayons. Apply a wash of black acrylic or watercolor paint.

FAUX PLASTER

Stir cornstarch into acrylic paint and apply an even coat on the paper. Etch a design in the wet paint with a fork or stylus.

GLITTER

Draw a design on the paper with white craft glue. Sprinkle glitter on the wet glue and let dry. Remove the excess glitter.

WET-ON-WET WATERCOLOR

Wet the paper with a sponge brush. Apply watercolor paint to the wet surface.

SPONGE MARBLE

Dip a sponge in paint and blot. Lightly pat the sponge on the paper.

SPRAY MARBLE

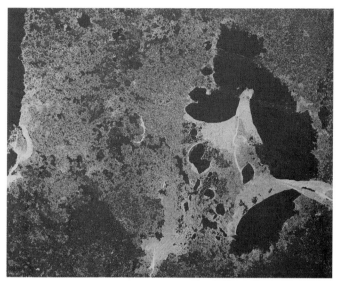

Fill a basin with water. Spray a thin film of spray paint on the surface of the water. Dip the paper in the water. Let dry.

DIP DYE

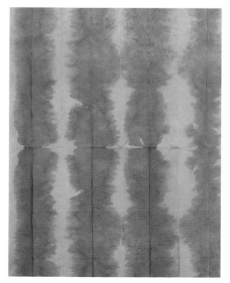

Fold tissue or mulberry paper in an accordion pattern. Wet the paper. Dip one side in diluted pink paint and the opposite in orange. Unfold and let dry.

SPONGE PAINT

Dip the sponge in paint and swirl it on the paper.

DRY SPLATTER

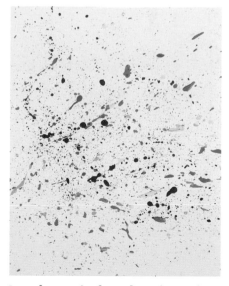

Load a paintbrush with acrylic paint. Hold it over the paper and tap it against the edge of a metal ruler.

WET-ON-WET SPLATTER

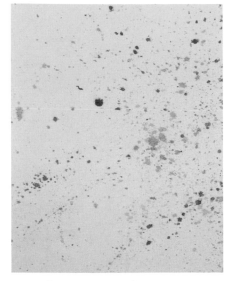

Wet the paper with a sponge brush. Load a paintbrush with watercolor paint. Hold it over the paper and tap it against the edge of a metal ruler.

DISTRESSED PAINT

Paint the paper with acrylic paint. Let dry. Sand with medium-grit sandpaper.

PAINT STENCIL

Dip a stencil brush in acrylic paint and blot on a paper towel. Fill in the exposed area of a stencil with short perpendicular strokes.

DISTRESSED INK

Crinkle the paper and dip it into diluted acrylic paint. Let dry. Lightly rub the ridges with a flat ink pad.

ANTIQUE STAMPING

Coat a paper towel with chalk and rub it on the paper. Stamp on the chalked paper.

MASKED STAMPING

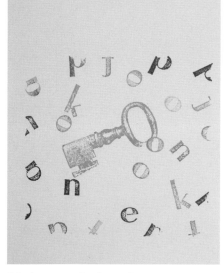

Make a window from scrap paper. Place it on the paper and stamp within the window and overlapping the edge of the window.

REVERSE STAMPING

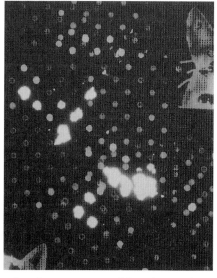

Dip the stamp in bleach and blot slightly. Press the stamp on dark paper. The bleach will draw the color from the paper.

PIPE CLEANER STAMPING

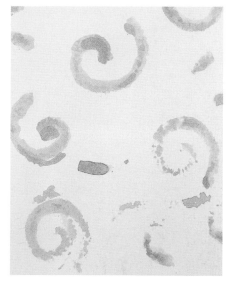

Bend short lengths of pipe cleaners into curved shapes. Dip them in diluted acrylic paint and press them on the paper.

CHALK STENCIL

Rub a sponge dauber in scrapbook chalk and use it to fill in the exposed area of a stencil.

CHALK

Rub the flat side of scrapbook chalk over the paper in a random pattern.

PULLED PAINT

Drop paint along the top edge of the paper. Press the edge of a cardboard scrap over the paint and pull down. Move it back and forth to make scallops.

PUNCHING

Rockets, radishes, robots, race cars, rabbits, roses . . . You can get punch drunk on the array of punch designs that are available. Yet, you don't need lots of paper punches to incorporate paper punching techniques into your crafting. Some very interesting effects can be created by simply punching multiple holes with a standard, small, round-hole punch. Look for other punches that can be used in creative ways, and add them to your collection over time. Punch art is fast and foolproof, and punches provide an easy way to make multiple images.

Punching

It is also possible to create design and texture with a handheld single-hole punch. We can thank Benjamin Smith of Massachusetts, who in 1885 invented this tool specifically for train conductors to use for punching passengers' tickets. His spring-loaded punch had a built-in receptacle for collecting the waste paper confetti, and thereby keeping the floors of passenger trains squeaky clean.

The one design limitation shared with both specialty punches and hand-held punches is that their design allows you to punch only the edges and not the interiors of the paper shapes.

Medium- and light-weight papers work best for punching. Avoid fibrous papers such as mulberry and rice paper because the embedded strands will prevent you from achieving a clean edge.

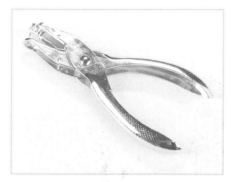

This is the punch that our grandparents grew up with and it can still serve as a handy and versatile tool.

Punching Projects

STARRY NIGHT

Poke holes in the night sky to reveal a snowy white backdrop.

YOU WILL NEED

- artwork with a night sky
- paper punch (small hole)
- paper punch (large hole)

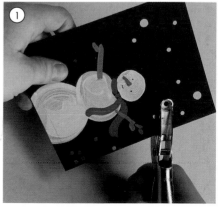

① Punch holes in a random pattern in the background of the artwork with both punches.

TODAY YOU ARE TWO

A punch will outline an important number or letter. Use velveteen paper, which will not crease when rolled, and work from the outside to the inside.

YOU WILL NEED

- 2⅝" x 4" (6.7 x 10.2 cm) rectangle of velveteen paper
- paper punch (small circle)
- pencil

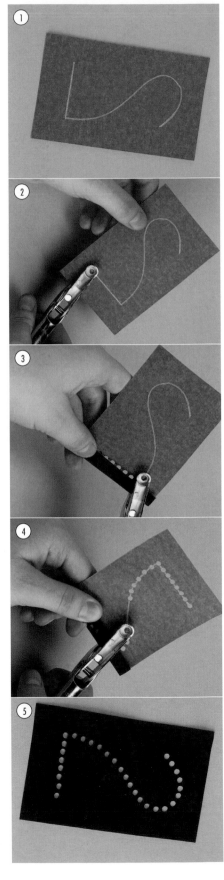

① On the wrong side of the paper, draw the number in reverse.

② Starting at the bottom edge, punch holes along the marked line.

③ Carefully roll the edge to continue punching.

④ Repeat by punching near the opposite edge and working toward the center.

⑤ Unroll the paper and flatten.

STIPPLED OVAL

Here's a bright idea. Punch holes that radiate from the cut edge of a silhouette shape.

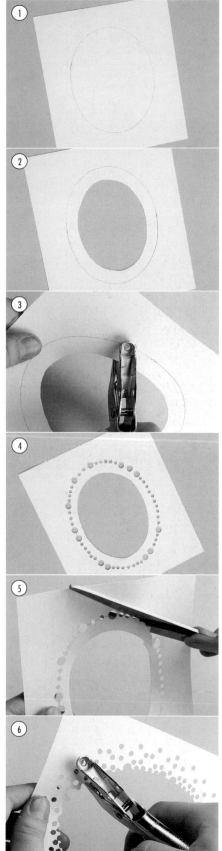

YOU WILL NEED

- paper of the desired size and shape
- pencil
- scissors
- paper punch (small hole)
- paper punch (large hole)

① Draw an oval on the wrong side of the paper.

② Cut the center from the oval to within ½" (1.3 cm) of the marked line.

③ Punch along the marked line with both punches.

④ Punch along the entire marked line.

⑤ Cut along the marked line.

⑥ Working from the center out, punch in a random pattern.

COLOR BLOCK FLOWERS

Colorful squares accentuate the beauty of the punch pattern.

YOU WILL NEED

- collection of coordinating colored paper
- scrap of colored paper
- note card
- double-sided adhesive
- novelty punch
- scissors

① Punch two rows of images in the scrap paper.

② Cut squares from the coordinating papers that are slightly larger than the image.

③ Arrange them on the note card to correspond with the image windows, and attach them with the double-sided adhesive.

④ Attach the punched paper to the note card with the double-sided adhesive.

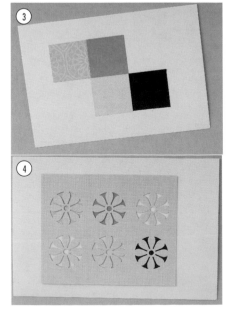

SWAN

For subtle texture, punch an all-over pattern within a simple shape. Then back it with paper that is one shade lighter or darker.

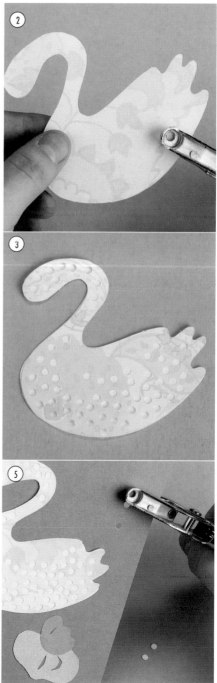

YOU WILL NEED

- template #1, page 178
- print paper
- white paper
- tracing paper
- pencil
- scraps of paper in the following colors: lavender, gold, and avocado
- note card
- spray adhesive
- scissors
- paper punch (small hole)

① Cut out the swan shapes from the print paper, using the templates as guides.

② Punch an all-over pattern in the swan body shape.

③ Cut a matching shape from the white paper. Spray the front of the white swan with adhesive and press the punched swan in place on top.

④ Noting overlaps, attach the swan and flower shapes to the note card.

⑤ Punch vertical lines in the background.

DINNER PARTY

Typical of novelty punches is a delicate design spotlighting a tiny knife, fork, and spoon.

YOU WILL NEED

- small square of colored paper
- scrap of coordinating paper
- note card
- novelty punch
- adhesive

① Punch image in the paper scrap. Attach it to a note card with a small strip of coordinating paper.

FALL FOLIAGE CARD

An array of warm autumn papers makes a beautiful leafy rainbow.

YOU WILL NEED

- collection of coordinating colored papers
- novelty punch
- blank greeting card

① Punch images from the papers. Arrange and attach them to the card in the desired order.

CROWN TAG

Accentuate the positive and the negative. Post both on a dark gift tag.

YOU WILL NEED

- small square of colored paper
- paper tag
- novelty punch
- double-sided adhesive

① Punch images in the paper scrap. Attach one solid image and the punched square to the tag with the double-sided adhesive.

① Punch holes at each scallop.

② Pierce holes around each punched hole.

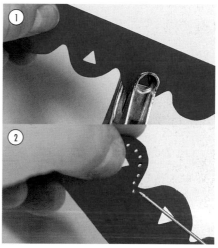

PAPER LACE BORDER

Pierced and punched vellum creates paper lace that invites a closer look. This fast and easy project requires two tools and two steady hands.

① Cut an irregular starburst shape from the lightweight paper.

② Punch lines along the rays.

DIAMOND RING

Draw starbursts with a paper punch and increase the wow factor of a heart-felt message.

PAPER PIECING

Paper piecing is the paper crafter's solution to illustration. Born from scrapbook art, it consists of arranging individual shapes to make an image or design. It brings to mind silk screen and paint-by-number art because of similar areas of solid color that are combined for a whole. Also similar to fabric appliqué work, areas that would appear in the background are positioned first, followed by pieces that would appear in the foreground. Each new layer slightly overlaps the previous layer, adding visual depth. Shading and outlining are limited because they require cutting separate paper shapes.

Paper Piecing Projects

To make the shapes, transfer the templates to the desired colored papers. Overlapping edges are indicated with the broken lines. Choose solid colored papers or those with small patterns. Also combine hues and values with enough contrast to define the design. Choose adhesives from the chart on page 7.

T-REX

General directions for paper piecing

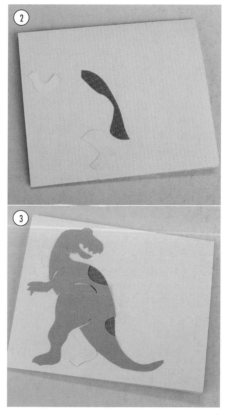

YOU WILL NEED

- template #2, page 181
- papers in the desired colors
- adhesives

① Cut out the shapes and assemble them in order on the craft table.

② Adhere the bottom layer of shapes to the page.

③ Adhere the remaining shapes in place.

④ Add hand-drawn or hand-painted accents to the pieces before they are layered and secured to the background.

TIP ✂

Note that you can lightly mark the background with a pencil for shape placement. Erase any marks after all of the pieces have been glued in place.

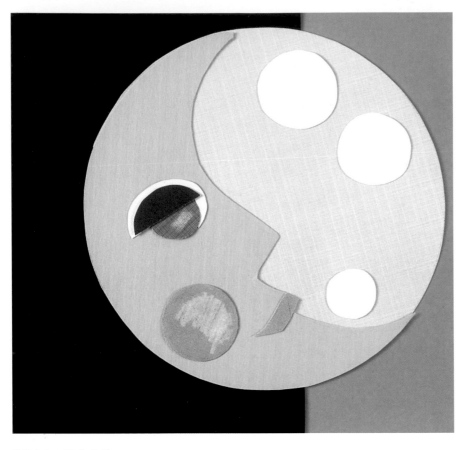

FULL MOON
template #3, page 181

WHO'S THERE?

template #4, page 180

AIR MAIL

IT'S A PARTY PARDNER!

template #5, page 180

APRIL SHOWERS

you're invited

template #6, page 181

SUMMER OF LOVE

template #7, page 178

CHERUB PAIR

you must have been
a beautiful baby

template #8, page 179

FLORETS

templates #9, 10, and 11, pages 179 and 180

FOLDING

If you have experience with turning paper scraps into airplanes or converting gum wrappers into necklaces, you have all the training needed to become a folding phenom. Pieces presented include everything from the frivolous to the practical. And don't be afraid to tackle more complex projects. Start with the envelope or the pocket, and work your way up to the origami flower. The weight of the paper may be important to the strength or to the bulk of individual projects. Weights are recommended for nonspecific papers in the materials lists.

Folding Projects

SPOKED FLOWER

As easy as 1-2-3, but without the 3.
All it takes is 1, cut and 2, fold.

YOU WILL NEED

- template #12, page 174
- 5" (12.7 cm) square of two-tone paper (medium weight)
- tracing paper
- pencil
- scissors

1. Cut one flower shape, using the template as a guide.

2. Working clockwise, fold the petals up along the dotted line.

3. Tuck the corner of the last petal under the adjoining corner of the first to secure.

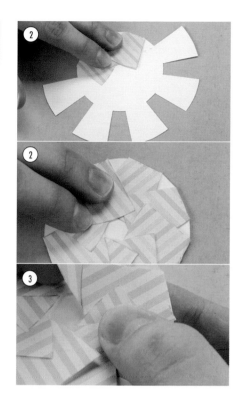

YO-YO FLOWER

Beloved by quilters everywhere, this folded blossom resembles a puckery cloth yo-yo.

YOU WILL NEED

- template #13, page 175
- 5" (12.7 cm) square of two-tone paper (medium weight)
- tracing paper
- pencil
- scissors

1. Cut one flower shape, using the template as a guide.

2. Working clockwise, fold the petals up along the dotted line.

3. Tuck the corner of the last petal under the adjoining corner of the first to secure.

4. Fold the corners back along the dotted line.

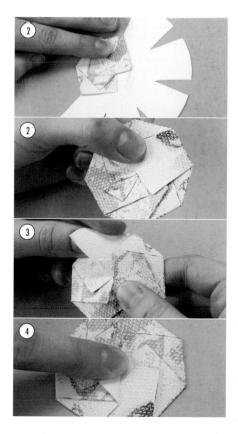

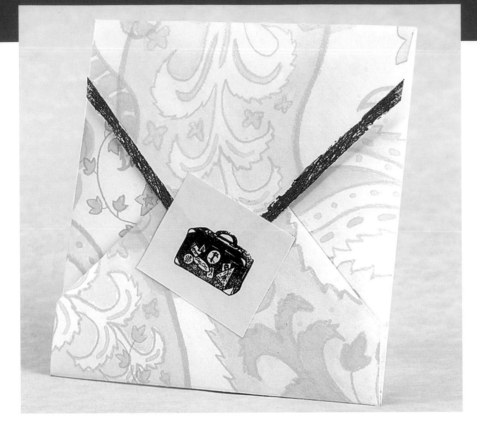

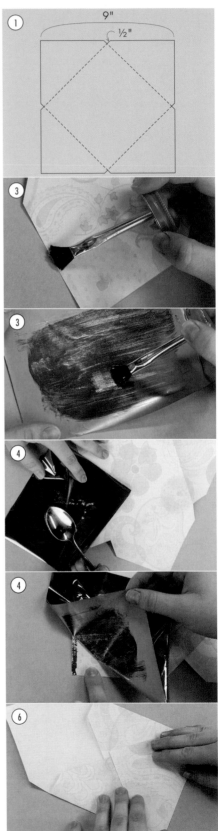

THE ENVELOPE PLEASE

An elegant envelope often says more than what is inside.
Sporting a gilded edge, this one will never go out of style.

YOU WILL NEED

- 12" x 12" (30.5 x 30.5 cm) sheet of scrapbook paper (light to medium weight)
- tracing paper
- rubber cement
- gilding film
- scissors
- double-sided adhesive
- decorative paper accent
- scoring tool
- spoon
- metal ruler
- pencil

① Cut one envelope shape, using the diagram as a guide.

② Score along the dotted lines.

③ Apply a thin strip of rubber cement along the sides of one flap. Apply rubber cement to the wrong side of the gilding film. Allow it to dry.

④ Place the film on the strips and rub with the flat side of a spoon. Remove from the paper.

⑤ Fold the side flaps in.

⑥ Fold the bottom flap up.

⑦ To seal the envelope, attach the decorative paper accent to the back with the double-sided adhesive.

PLEATED POCKET

Nothing is handier than a pocket on a shirt, or in this case a pocket
on a postcard. Use it to deliver a ticket, a dollar bill, or a gift card
to someone special.

YOU WILL NEED

- note card
- 6" x 8" (15.2 x 20.3 cm) sheet of two-tone paper (light to medium weight)
- double-sided adhesive

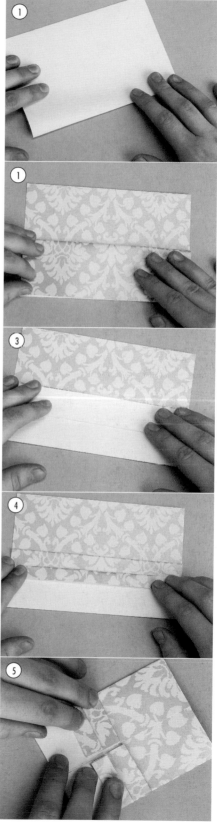

① Fold the bottom of the paper up to meet the top.

② Fold the upper edge of the top layer down to the fold line.

③ Fold the lower edge of the top layer up to the fold line.

④ Fold the upper edge of the top layer down to the fold line.

⑤ Place face-down and fold the sides to the center back.

⑥ Attach the pocket to the note card with the double-sided adhesive.

COLONIAL WINDOW

Open the window and pull up the sash to reveal a paper charm on a Merry Christmas note card.

YOU WILL NEED

- template #14, page 175
- 5" x 6" (12.7 x 15.2 cm) rectangle of two-tone paper (medium to heavy weight)
- tracing paper
- pencil
- note card
- paper charm
- double-sided adhesive
- adhesive-backed gem
- scoring tool
- metal ruler
- craft knife
- cutting mat

① Cut one window shape using the template as a guide. Also cut the solid horizontal and vertical lines as indicated on the template.

② Align the ruler at the ends of the horizontal cuts and score.

③ Fold the flaps open at the scored lines.

④ Attach the window to the note card with the double-sided adhesive. Center the paper charm in the window and attach it with the double-sided adhesive. Stick the gem to the top of the window.

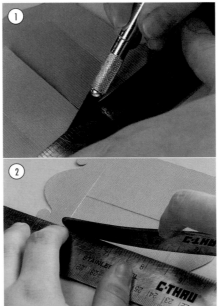

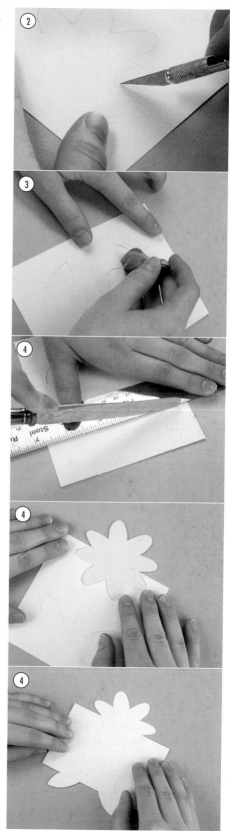

TRI-FOLD FLOWER

This folded flower is a graceful addition to a gift card. Use two-tone paper to make it pop from the page.

① Draw the flower and leaf outlines on the wrong side of the paper, using the template as a guide.

② Use the craft knife to cut along the marked lines.

③ Carefully erase the marked lines.

④ Score along the dotted lines and fold the flaps to the back.

YOU WILL NEED

- template #15, page 177
- 4¼" x 6" (10.8 x 15.2 cm) rectangle of two-tone paper (medium weight)
- tracing paper
- pencil
- craft knife
- cutting mat
- kneaded rubber eraser
- metal ruler
- scoring tool

YOU WILL NEED

- template #16, page 182
- 5" x 7" (12.7 x 17.8 cm) rectangle of two-tone paper (light to medium weight)
- tracing paper
- pencil
- craft knife
- cutting mat

① Cut one tree shape, using the template as a guide. Cut the V shapes along the marked lines.

② Fold the cut points down.

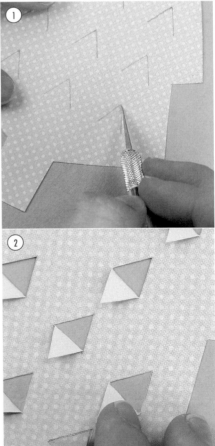

PEEK-A-BOO CHRISTMAS TREE

V shapes are cut and folded to cast lacy shadows on a polka-dot tree.

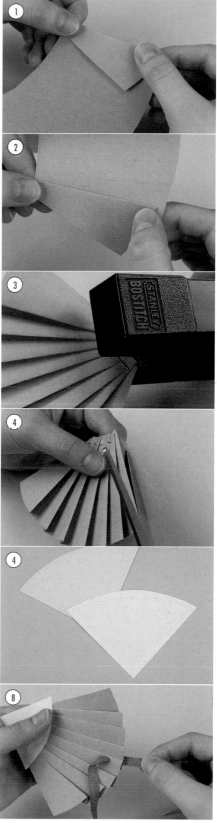

FAN ORNAMENT

The lowly paper fan is dressed up enough to hang as an exquisite ornament. Assemble eclectic papers and make an assortment of fancy fans.

YOU WILL NEED

- templates #17, page 174
- 8½" x 11" (21.6 x 27.9 cm) sheet of light-weight paper
- scraps of coordinating paper
- double-sided adhesive
- tracing paper
- pencil
- ribbon
- stapler
- paper punch
- scissors

① Cut one fan shape, using the template as a guide.

② Start with the right edge and fold in an accordion pattern along the dotted line.

③ Staple at the bottom through all layers.

④ On the wrong side of the fan, trim away the folded edges to reduce bulk.

⑤ Cut two wedge-shaped bases from the coordinating paper. Cut two pieces of double-sided adhesive that are slightly smaller than the wedge and attach them to the backs of shapes.

⑥ Attach one base shape to the bottom of the fan. Attach the second shape on the reverse side.

⑦ Punch a hole in the top of the fan.

⑧ Thread the ribbon through the hole.

⑨ Tie a knot and trim the ribbon ends.

HAPPY BIRTHDAY!

RICRAC BORDER

Follow the twists and turns, keep your folds at right angles, and enjoy the ride.

YOU WILL NEED

- ¾" x 12" (1.9 x 30.5 cm) strip of two-tone paper (medium weight)
- scissors

① Place the strip on the craft table with the wrong side up.

② Fold in the center at a right angle.

③ Fold under again to create a point.

④ Fold the right end up.

⑤ Fold the left end up.

⑥ Turn the paper over and fold the right end up.

⑦ Fold the left end up.

⑧ Turn the paper over and fold the right end to the right side.

⑨ Fold the left end to the left side.

⑩ Continue to complete the border design and trim the ends.

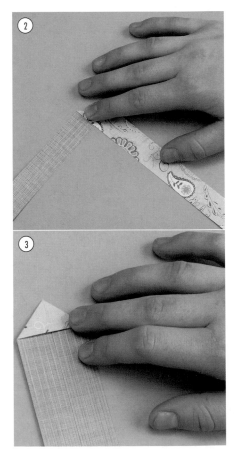

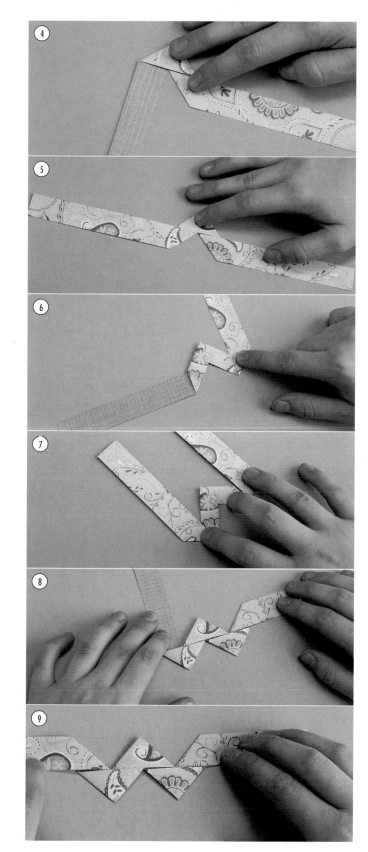

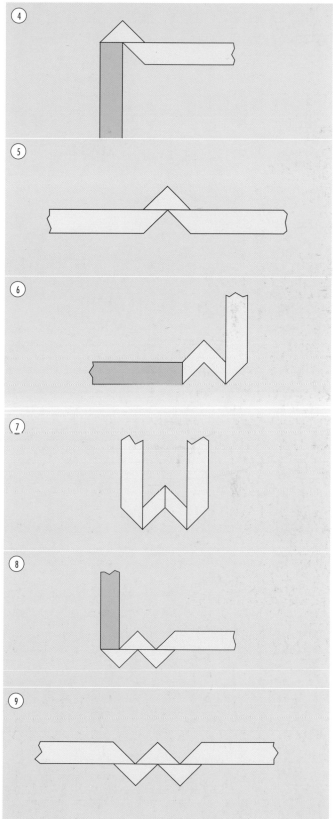

FRETWORK BORDER

Two V shapes mark the spot. Use this two-tone border on greeting cards, scrapbook pages, or a journal cover.

YOU WILL NEED

- two ½" x 12" (1.3 x 30.5 cm) strips of two-tone paper (medium weight)
- scissors

① Place the strip on the craft table with the right side up.

② Fold the left end down at 1" (2.5 cm).

③ Turn the paper over and fold the long end over to make a point.

④ Turn the long end over again and make a second point.

⑤ Turn the paper over and fold the end up at 2" (5.1 cm).

⑥ Repeat steps 3 and 4.

⑦ Turn the paper over and fold the end up at 2" (5.1 cm).

⑧ Repeat steps 3 and 4 to complete the V shape.

⑨ Trim the long end.

⑩ Repeat to make a second V shape.

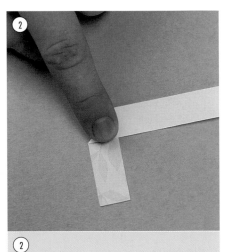

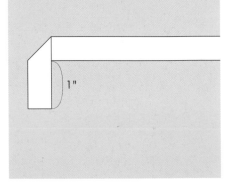

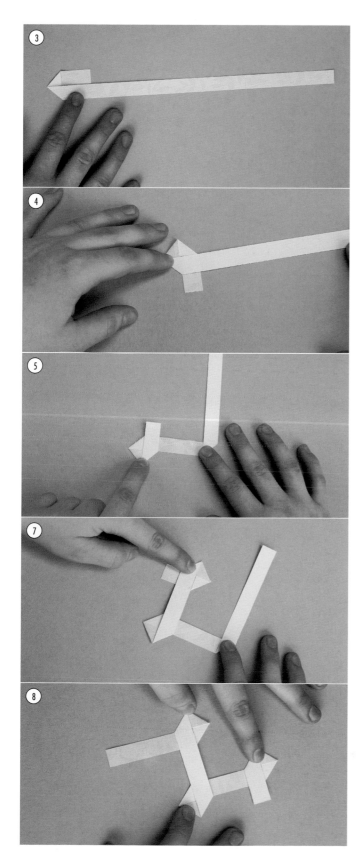

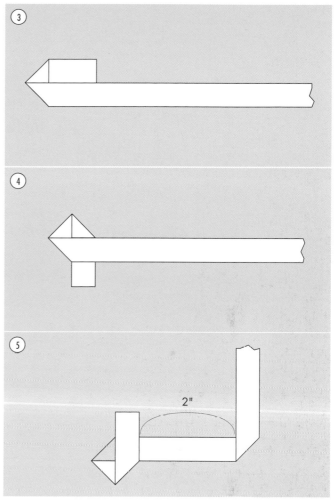

2"

MUFFIN CRADLE

A well-dressed muffin is irresistible for more than its delicious flavor. The container is equally enticing and can turn an ordinary brunch into a party.

YOU WILL NEED

- template #18, page 176
- 12" (30.5 cm) square sheet of two-tone paper (medium weight)
- tracing paper
- pencil
- double-sided adhesive
- 12" (30.5 cm) satin ribbon, ¼" (6 mm) wide
- scissors
- paper punch

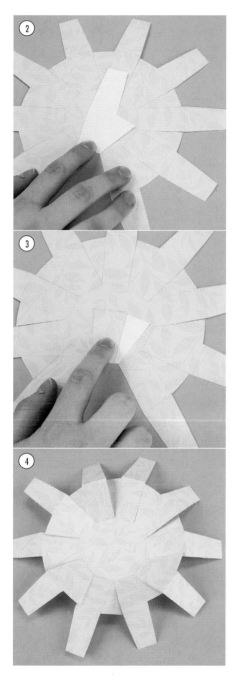

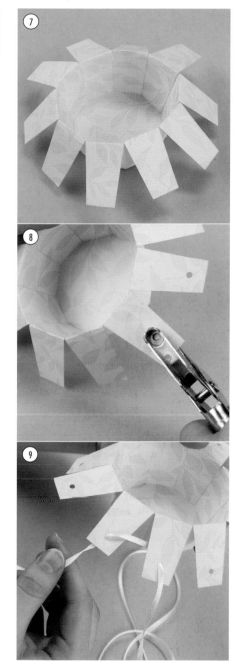

① Cut one cradle shape, using the template as a guide.

② Fold one section up at the inner dotted line.

③ Fold down at the center dotted line.

④ Fold the remaining sections.

⑤ Apply small squares of the double-sided adhesive in the pie shapes.

⑥ Remove the protective paper from one square to expose the adhesive. Align the cut edge of one section with the dotted line of the adjoining section and press together to join.

⑦ Repeat with the remaining sections.

⑧ Punch the end of each section.

⑨ Thread the ribbon through each hole.

⑩ Pull the ribbon ends to tighten and tie a bow. Trim the ribbon ends.

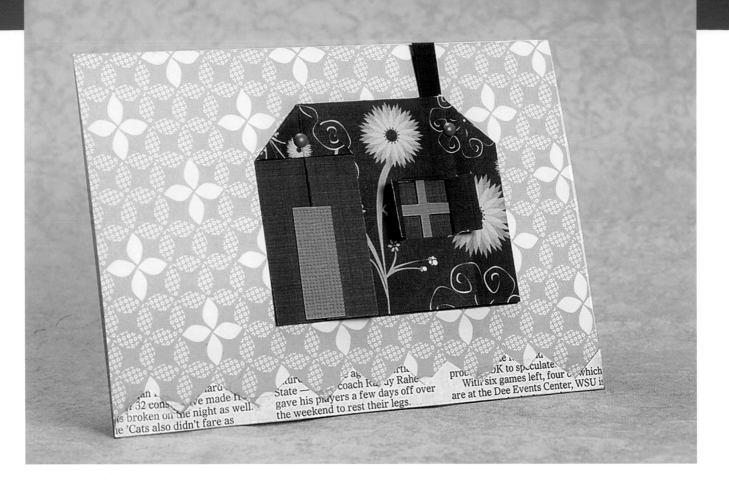

ORIGAMI SCHOOLHOUSE

This schoolhouse rocks! (and it's perfect for communicating good wishes to a favorite teacher).

YOU WILL NEED

- templates #19, page 197
- 3¼" x 5¼" (8.3 x 13.3 cm) rectangle of two-tone paper (medium weight)
- small scraps of coordinating paper
- tracing paper
- pencil
- double-sided adhesive
- craft knife
- cutting mat
- metal ruler

① Fold the rectangle in half. Unfold.

② Use the craft knife to cut the slits as indicated on the diagram. Refold.

③ Fold the left side over at ⅝" (1.6 cm).

④ Fold the corner down at ⅝" (1.6 cm).

⑤ Fold open to make a gable.

⑥ Repeat steps 3 and 4 with the opposite corner.

⑦ Open and bend the point to the inside.

⑧ Cut a chimney, window grid, and door from the paper scraps, using the templates as guides.

⑨ Slide the chimney through the slit at the fold line and secure with double-sided adhesive. Center the grid behind the window slits and secure with double-sided adhesive.

⑩ Fold open the window shutters.

⑪ Attach the door with double-sided adhesive.

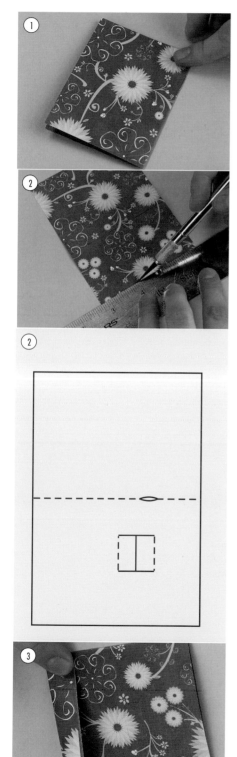

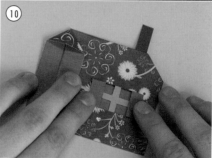

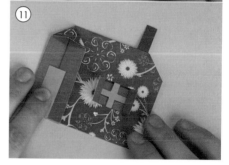

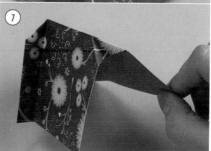

ORIGAMI FLOWER

The beauty of origami is in the transformation of a single square. Begin at square one and crease and crimp your way to lovely pleated petals.

① Fold the square from corner to corner twice to make an X. Unfold.

② Fold the corners to the center to make a diamond. Unfold.

③ Cut a slit from one corner to the center.

④ Fold back at the adjoining diagonal fold.

⑤ Align the fold at the corner of the diamond and crease.

⑥ Repeat steps 4 and 5 with the remaining two folded corners.

⑦ Bring a folded corner to the center, opening and refolding the upper layer; crease.

⑧ Repeat with the remaining two corners.

⑨ Fold the remaining points to the center.

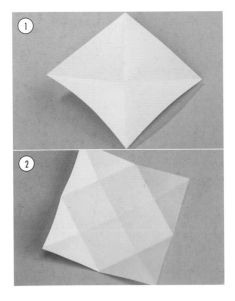

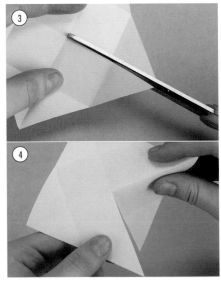

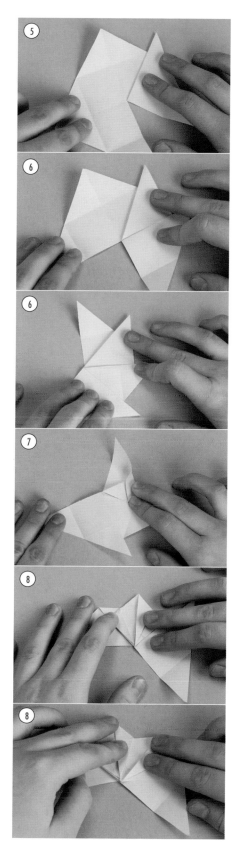

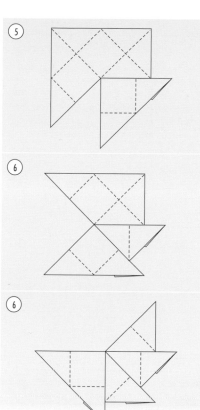

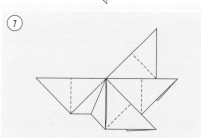

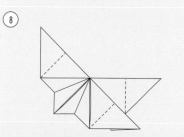

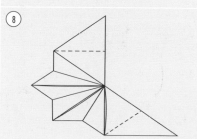

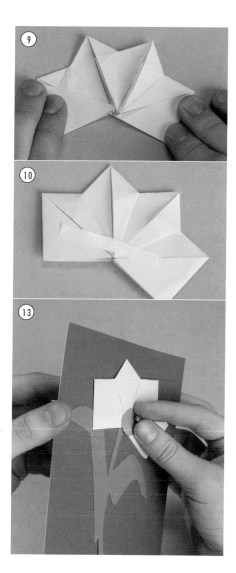

(10) Secure the layers with double-sided adhesive.

(11) Cut the stem and leaves from the coordinating paper, using the template as a guide.

(12) Attach the stem and leaves to the note card with the double-sided adhesive.

(13) Place the circle and the flower on the note card and use the craft knife to pierce through all layers. Insert and secure the brad.

③ Fold the corner down.

④ Repeat steps 2 and 3 with an adjoining corner.

⑤ Fold the adjoining point up.

⑥ Fold the top left corner down.

⑦ Fold the top right corner down slightly less than the left.

⑧ Fold in half.

⑨ Open and invert the upper half of the center fold.

⑩ Place on the craft table with the shorter wing on top. Fold back the top layer of the bottom corner.

⑪ Punch the top wing.

⑫ Cut the body from the coordinating paper, using the template.

⑬ Layer the wings and body on the note card and staple through all layers to secure.

ORIGAMI BUTTERFLY

A butterfly graces a simple note card. Scattered punched accents help make it lighter than air.

① Fold the square from corner to corner, then unfold. Repeat in the opposite direction to make an X.

② Fold one corner to the center.

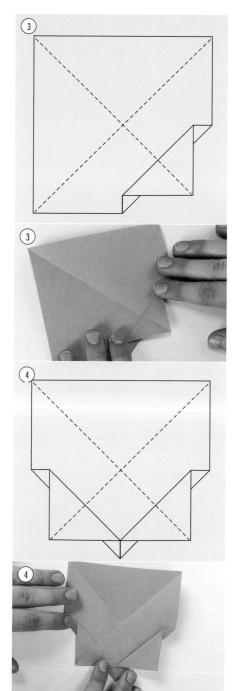

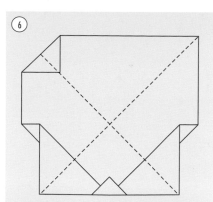

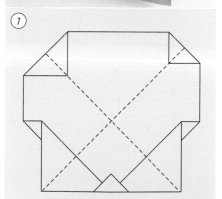

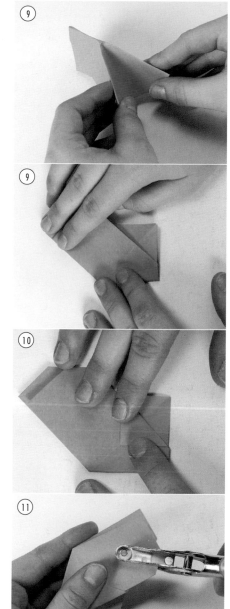

COLLAGE

Soon after paper was invented, artists found creative ways to use it. They cut intricate paper designs to adorn books of scripture and family history. Printed images were enhanced with gemstones, silk fibers, symbolic signs, and trims, a practice that has carried over to contemporary collage artists. The most famous modern collage artist is Henri Matisse. In 1930 he cut and arranged shapes to use as thumbnail sketches for larger oil paintings. Enamored with this process, he published a collection of his cut designs, celebrating his ability to "draw with scissors."

Specialty papers

**Choose from a large
assortment of papers.**

Bright chipboard boxes and
removable labels

Textured and embossed papers

Old children's books

Old photos and postcards

Recycled calendars and
greeting cards

Old magazines

Collage Projects

Representing a stripped-down form of collage, the featured projects are limited to paper and are offered as sample compositions.

The art in this art form is in the choice and placement of the backgrounds and images. Unlike the more direct method of painting, you can change the appearance of your design by arranging and re-arranging the elements until they are glued in place.

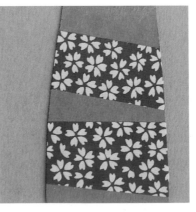

ZIP LINE BABY CARD

If you can't find just the right background paper, make your own with paint or markers.

THE JUGGLER

Catch someone's attention by adding detail to silhouette shapes.

PRINCE OF THE PICK-UP STICKS

When combining paper sticks to build a border, make them slightly off balance to boost interest.

HONEY, I'M HOME

Add whimsy by pairing images that are opposites.

HOTEL BRAEMORE CARD

Create the impression of an expanded frame by allowing selected images to bleed to the edges.

DINNER'S READY

To avoid a disaster and a collage do-over, write a caption or message on a separate piece of paper.

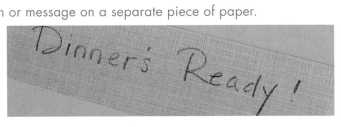

KING TOMATO

Packaging equals art. What better way to pay homage to your favorite food?

ACROSS THE MILES

You can age coordinating papers by scuffing them with fine sandpaper.

DANCE PARTY

To keep the eye moving around a composition, repeat one dominant element.

IT'S SPRING

You can't go wrong when you start with a strong central image and then place supporting elements around it.

KING OF THE KITCHEN CARD

Mixed-up scale and dissimilar art styles combine for an amusing card.

HERE THEY COME

The chase is on! Curves cut across a flat plane to suggest action and movement.

Here they come down the street.
Woo-ee! Woo-ee!

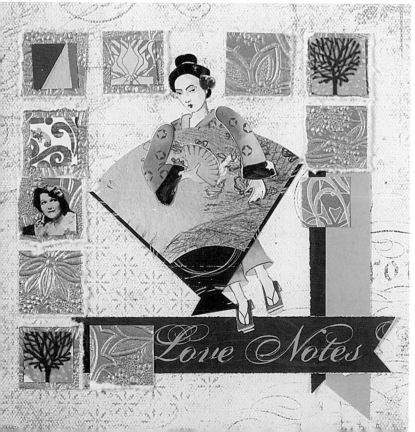

LOVE NOTES

Soften the look of a geometric border by layering bits and pieces on top of the blocks.

MOSAICS

Hooray! It is possible to make three-dimensional mosaics with two-dimensional paper. Traditional mosaics have a knobby appearance because they are built with individual tiles or pebbles. Make paper tiles with medium-weight paper, tissue paper, and even discarded cereal boxes and have fun imitating a serious art form that has truly stood the test of time.

Paper Tiles

There are different ways to transform paper into tiles for mosaics.

TISSUE PEBBLES

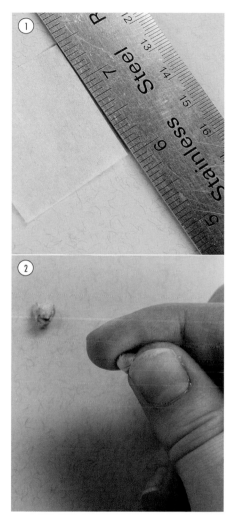

① Use scissors or a craft knife to cut 1½" (3.8 cm) squares.

② Roll each square between your fingers until it is compact.

③ Use white craft glue to stick the pebbles to the paper. For easy handling, pick up the pebbles individually with tweezers. In order to get defined shapes, the pebbles should be pressed tightly together. It is possible to reposition the pebbles before the glue dries.

MINI-TILES

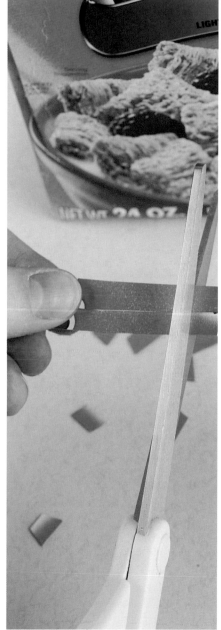

Make mini-tiles from the perfect paper— discarded cereal boxes. They are easy to cut with scissors, rigid enough to use with white craft glue, are printed in bright colors, and have a glossy finish.

SPIKY TILES

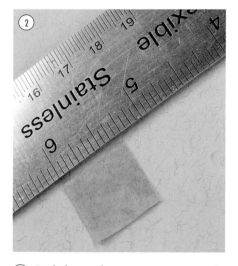

① Cut light-weight tissue or origami paper into ¾" (1.9 cm) squares.

② Fold the squares on the end of a narrow dowel.

Mosaic Projects

GRECIAN URN SCRAPBOOK PAGE

Make an antique in a hurry by securing paper bits with double-sided adhesive.

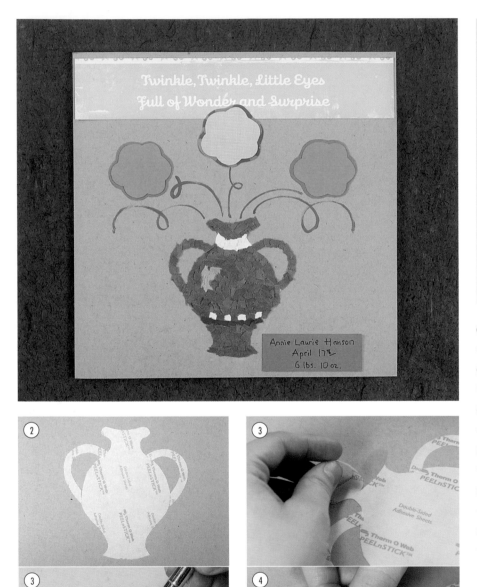

- medium-weight paper in selected colors
- scrapbook paper
- double-sided adhesive
- template #22, page 182
- tracing paper
- pencil
- decorative paper accents
- craft knife
- cutting mat

① Cut one urn from the double-sided adhesive, using the template as a guide.

② Remove the backing paper and press the urn on the scrapbook page.

③ Cut through the protective layer only at the desired break, and remove.

④ Place small squares of torn medium-weight paper on the exposed adhesive.

⑤ Repeat steps 3 and 4 for each color area.

⑥ Attach the decorative paper accents with the double-sided adhesive.

CAT ALBUM

I spy two little eyes on an album that will delight and amuse both cat lovers and paper lovers.

1. Draw the cat on the watercolor paper, using the template as a guide.
2. Make tissue pebbles from the tissue paper.
3. Work in small sections and glue the pebbles to the paper.
4. Let dry.

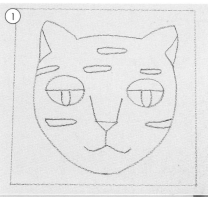

BUTTERFLY BOX

Make this gift box for an extra-special friend. It just may outshine the present that is tucked inside.

1. Draw the butterfly on the box top, using the template as a guide.
2. Make tissue pebbles from the tissue paper.
3. Work in small sections and glue the pebbles to the paper.
4. Let dry.

PLAQUE

An important message is outlined with festive tissue stripes.

YOU WILL NEED

- chipboard rectangle (medium weight)
- tissue paper in desired colors
- white craft glue
- scissors
- tweezers

① Cut windows in the chipboard to accommodate selected artwork.

② Make tissue pebbles from the tissue paper.

③ Work in small sections and glue the pebbles to the chipboard.

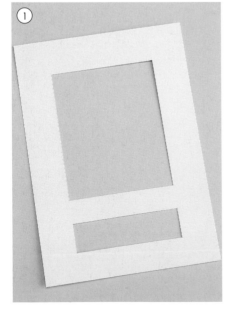

CHERRY BLOSSOM SHOES

Step up with torn strips and mosaic squares and you'll find that you can teach an old shoe new tricks. You can also decorate small oxfords with these techniques. Cover the toes with torn strips and the tongues with spiky frosting.

YOU WILL NEED

- pair of baby shoes
- torn strips of medium-weight paper
- ¾" (1.9 cm) squares of origami paper
- double-sided adhesive
- acrylic paint
- narrow dowel (⅛" or ⅜" [3 or 5 mm] wide)
- paintbrush

① Cover the toe with double-sided adhesive.

② Remove the protective paper to expose the adhesive.

③ Leaving the top of the adhesive exposed (approximately ⅜" [1 cm]), press the strips of paper on the shoe. For optimal coverage, overlap the strips along the sides.

④ Fold one square around the dowel end.

⑤ Press the dowel end on the adhesive. Repeat to cover the exposed adhesive.

⑥ Paint the sides, back, and strap of the shoe. Let dry.

⑦ Repeat steps 1 through 6 for the remaining shoe.

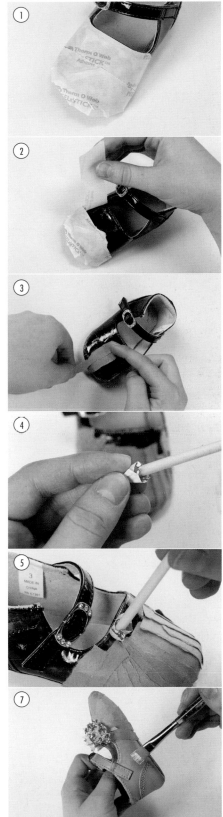

FAUX GROUT MINIFRAME

The nattiness of this mini picture frame makes the case for recycling.
A dab of black paint adds just the right amount of contrast.

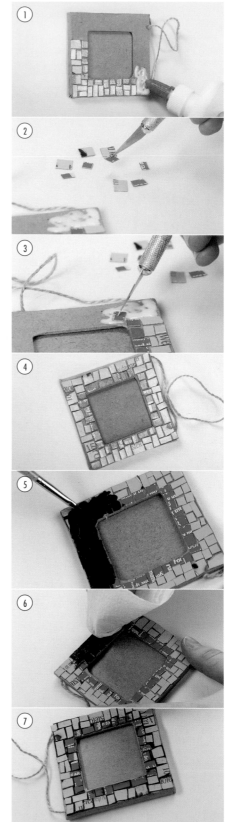

YOU WILL NEED

- chipboard frame
- tiles cut from cereal boxes (squares and rectangles approximately ¼" to ³∕₈" [6 mm to 1 cm] wide)
- white craft glue
- black acrylic paint
- craft knife
- paintbrush
- paper napkins

① Apply small areas of glue to the frame.

② Pick up a tile with the point of the craft knife.

③ Place the tile on the glue.

④ Cover the surface area and let dry.

⑤ Apply small areas of black paint. Make sure to get the paint in the recesses between the tiles.

⑥ With the napkin, rub the excess paint off of the tiles.

⑦ Work your way around the frame; let dry.

GOLD DUST MINIFRAME

Made from a discarded box, this frame is topped with gold
embossing powder.

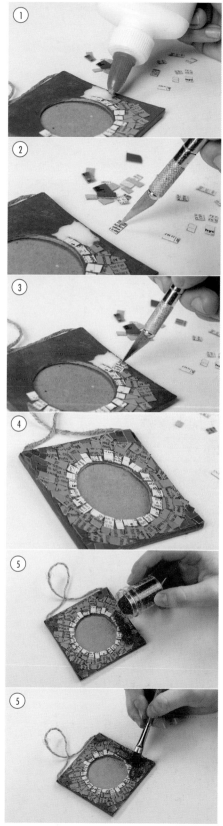

YOU WILL NEED

- painted frame
- tiles cut from cereal boxes
  (triangles and rectangles
  approximately ¼" to ⅜"
  [6 mm to 1 cm] wide)
- white craft glue
- gold embossing powder
- crafter's heat gun
- craft knife
- soft paintbrush

① Apply small areas of glue to
the frame.

② Pick up a tile with the point of the
craft knife.

③ Place the tile on the glue.

④ Cover the surface area and let dry.

⑤ Sprinkle powder on the frame.
With the brush, push the powder
between the tiles.

⑥ Following manufacturer's directions,
apply heat to the powder to solidify.

GIFT BOX

What curiosity a well-dressed package kindles. Make one with a paper topping that looks like a sweet confection.

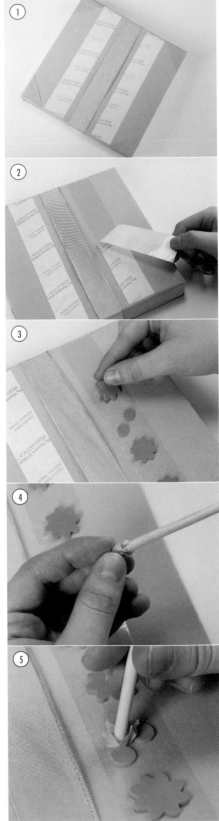

YOU WILL NEED

- wrapped gift box
- double-sided adhesive
- foam flowers and polka dots
- pink and yellow tissue paper cut into 1" (2.5 cm) square
- narrow dowel (1/8" or 3/16" [3 or 5 mm] wide)

① Cut strips of double-sided adhesive to fit the top of the box.

② Remove the protective paper from one strip to expose the adhesive.

③ Press the foam shapes to the adhesive.

④ Fold one tissue paper square around the dowel end.

⑤ Press the dowel end on the adhesive. Repeat to cover the exposed adhesive.

⑥ Repeat steps 1 through 5 for the remaining strip of adhesive.

⑦ Cover any exposed adhesive with strips of tissue.

CHUNKY TILES SCRAPBOOK PAGE

In a former life these avant-garde tiles were old news
(that is, printed on old newspapers).

YOU WILL NEED

- molded paper dough (page 170)
- wax paper
- acrylic paint
- scrapbook paper
- white craft glue
- rolling pin
- pencil
- paintbrush
- craft knife

① Roll the paper dough between two sheets of wax paper to ³⁄₈" to ¼" (3 to 6 mm) thick.

② Allow the paper to dry completely, and paint with desired colors of acrylic paint. Let dry.

③ Break the paper into the small irregular tiles.

④ Draw a picture frame on the paper.

⑤ Apply a thin layer of white craft glue to a small area of the frame.

⑥ Pick up a tile with the craft knife and press it into the glue.

⑦ Repeat steps 5 and 6 to cover the frame with tiles; let dry.

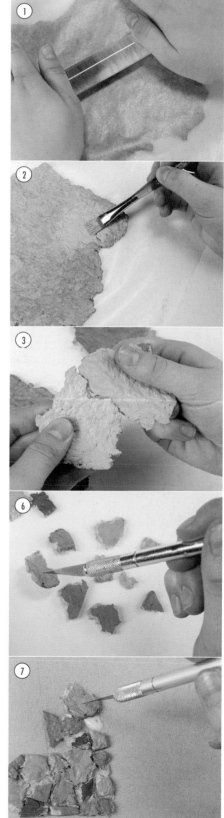

WEAVING

Because paper is a great substitute for fiber, your kindergarten teacher was inspired when she showed you how to weave construction paper into place mats. Paper requires no loom or additional support system, it is flexible, and it can be used for both warp and weft. Paper allows for variations of the basic over/under weaving method, such as working in a circular pattern or entwining curved shapes to make an interesting silhouette.

Weaving Projects

ENVELOPES

Good things come in small envelopes. Make a few slits in the
edge of this envelope and then weave in bright paper bands.
The glue on the underside of the flap serves as the finish to
seal the edge in place.

YOU WILL NEED
- envelopes, large and small
- lightweight decorative paper
- pencil
- metal ruler
- scissors

Small envelope

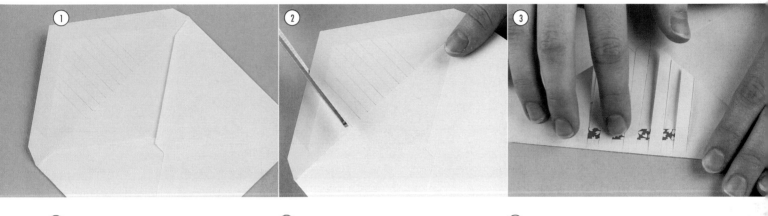

① On the inside of the flap, draw lines
that are perpendicular to the flap fold,
from the fold to the diagonal edges.

② Cut slits in the flap at the marked lines.

③ Cut paper strips ¼" (6 mm) wide.
Weave the paper strips in an alternat-
ing pattern.

Large envelope

① On the inside of the flap, draw
lines that are perpendicular to the
diagonal edges.

② Cut along the marked lines.

③ Cut paper strips, and weave them
through the slits along the edges.

miracles still happen.

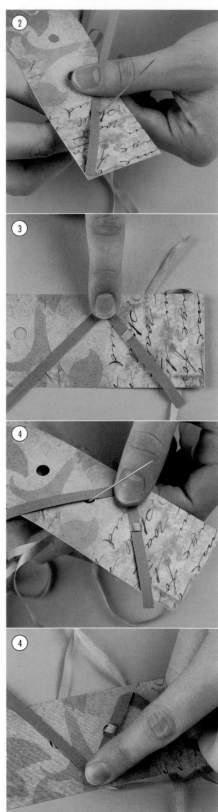

JAGGED BORDER

Anchor a narrow band of paper with contrasting ribbon. Then pinch at uneven angles to make a border that is flat-out fabulous.

YOU WILL NEED

- 1¾" x 12" (4.5 x 30.5 cm) strip of paper
- three ³/₁₆" x 12" (0.5 x 30.5 cm) strips of coordinating paper
- silk ribbon
- large eye needle
- cellophane tape
- scissors
- paper punch (large hole)

① Punch holes 1" (2.5 cm) apart in the wide strip.

② Place one narrow strip over the first hole. Make a loop through the hole with the ribbon to secure the strip.

③ Place the strips on the craft table and fold the strip at an angle.

④ Repeat steps 2 and 3 to complete the border.

⑤ Trim the ribbon ends and tape them to the back of the border.

CAGEY SCRAPBOOK PAGE

Cut a few horizontal slits and make the cage for this
canary part of the page.

YOU WILL NEED

- template #25, page 177
- scrap of yellow paper
- scrap of coordinating paper
- scrapbook paper
- tracing paper
- double-sided adhesive
- cellophane tape
- decorative paper accents
- pencil
- metal ruler
- craft knife
- cutting mat

①　Cut the bird and cage outline from the paper scraps, using the template as a guide.

②　Place the cage outline on the page and mark around the inside edge. Cut horizontal lines within the marked line.

③　Attach the bird to the center of the cage with the double-sided adhesive.

④　Cut narrow strips from the scraps that are at least 5" (12.7 cm) long. Weave the strips through the slits in a random pattern. Note that the strips should be placed over the bird.

⑤　Trim the ends.

⑥　Tape the ends on the wrong side of the paper.

⑦　Attach the cage outline to the page with the double-sided adhesive.

⑧　Attach the decorative paper accents with the double-sided adhesive.

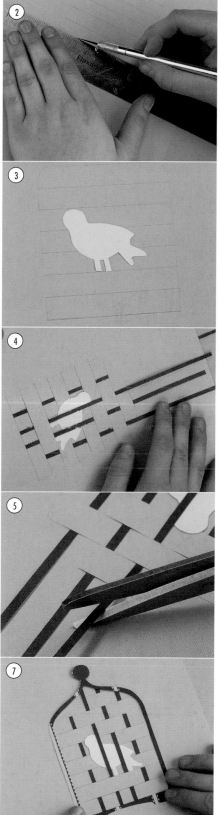

BRICK BORDER SCRAPBOOK PAGE

Basic zigzag papers combine to make a border that is anything but basic.

YOU WILL NEED

- 2" x 12" (5.1 x 30.5 cm) strip of print paper (medium weight)
- 2" x 12" (5.1 x 30.5 cm) strip of coordinating print paper (medium weight)
- template #26, page 183
- tracing paper
- pencil
- scissors
- craft knife
- cutting mat

1. Cut zigzag shapes from the paper strips, using the template as a guide.

2. Starting at the bottom, wind the strips around each other to join.

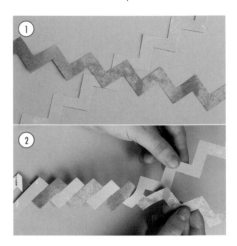

TWO HALVES VASE

Curved strips merge to make a simple paper vase with graceful contours.

YOU WILL NEED

- 4" x 6" (10.2 x 15.2 cm) rectangle of paper (medium weight)
- contrasting 4" x 6" (10.2 x 15.2 cm) rectangle of paper (medium weight)
- template #27, page 183
- scissors
- cellophane tape

1. Cut two mirror image vase shapes, using the template as a guide.

2. Weave the shapes together and tape the back to secure.

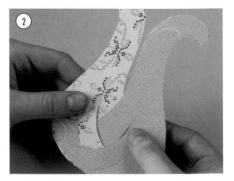

cycling through
the Vermont
countryside,
with Sam -
April 17, 2009

SPRINGTIME

I will keep
this day
in my **heart**
forever.

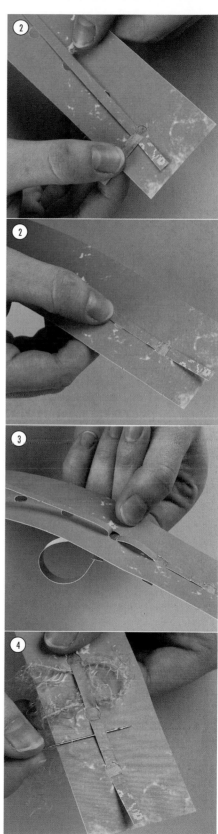

FUZZY WUZZY BORDER

Slide paper stays over a narrow strip to allow it to float on the surface of the paper. Use a needle to make loops of downy fiber.

YOU WILL NEED

- 1¾" x 12" (4.5 x 30.5 cm) strip of paper
- ³/₁₆" x 12" (0.19 x 30.5 cm) strip of matching paper
- twelve ³/₁₆" x 12" (0.5 x 30.5 cm) tabs of contrasting paper
- fuzzy yarn
- cellophane tape
- paper punch (large hole)
- needle

① Punch holes 1" (2.5 cm) apart in the wide strip.

② Place the narrow strip over the holes. Weave one tab over the narrow strip and through the holes to secure.

③ Repeat through all holes. On the back of the strip, tape the tab ends to secure.

④ Weave the yarn back and forth along the length of the strip.

WAVE SCRAPBOOK PAGE

Shake off the right angles of traditional weaving by incorporating weft papers that bring to mind the movement of ocean waves.

YOU WILL NEED

- 12" x 12" (30.5 x 30.5 cm) sheet of scrapbook paper (medium to heavy weight)
- assorted coordinating scrapbook paper (light to medium weight)
- double-sided adhesive
- pencil
- metal ruler
- scissors

① Mark a horizontal line 1" (2.5 cm) from the top of the page. Cut and remove narrow strips (approximately 1/16" [1.6 mm]) in a wavy pattern from the bottom edge to the marked line.

② From coordinating scrapbook papers, cut horizontal strips that match straight and contour edges. Arrange them on the craft table in descending order.

③ Weave the first strip in an over/under pattern.

④ Weave in the remaining strips. Use double-sided adhesive to attach a narrow strip along the bottom to secure the ends.

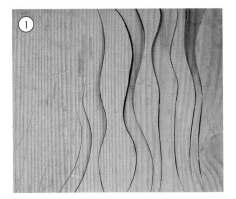

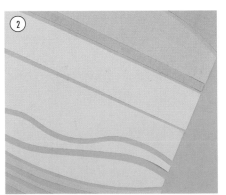

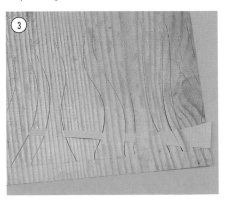

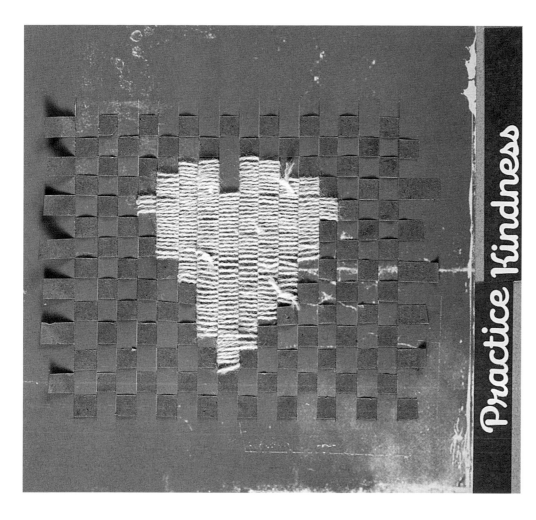

YARN HEART

A tactile yarn heart sits within a traditional checkerboard square.

Practice Kindness

YOU WILL NEED

- 6" x 6" (15.2 x 15.2 cm) square of paper
- ¼" x 5" (6 mm x 12.7 cm) strips of coordinating paper
- fine yarn
- craft knife
- pencil
- cutting mat
- metal ruler
- needle

① Cut lines that are ¼" (6 mm) apart in the center of the square.

② Draw a heart on the paper. Note that the heart will be used only to block out an area for the yarn weaving. The finished heart will be crude.

③ Weave the yarn over and under the slits within the marked area. When you run out of yarn, knot and trim the ends.

④ Weave the paper strips through the slits around the heart to fill in the background.

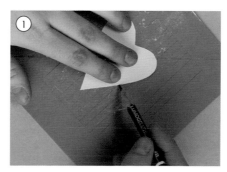

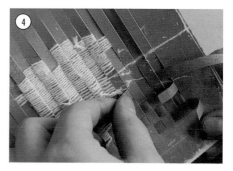

FLOWER

Run circles around boring die cuts by weaving in a circular pattern.
Paper and yarn form the weft that makes a bright flower even brighter.

YOU WILL NEED

- 4" x 6" (10.2 x 15.2 cm) rectangle of yellow paper
- template #28, page 183
- ¼" x 5" (6 mm x 12.7 cm) strip of print paper
- tracing paper
- pencil
- cellophane tape
- yarn

① Cut the flower shape, using the template as a guide.

② Weave the paper strip around the petals.

③ Weave the yarn around the petals.

④ Trim the ends and tape them to the back of the flower.

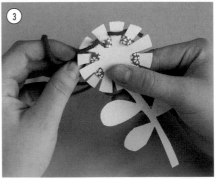

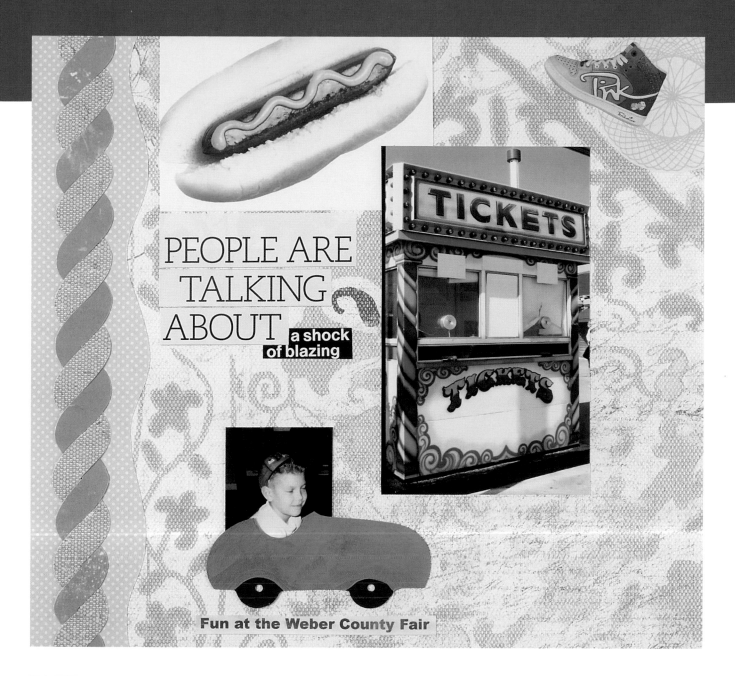

PEOPLE ARE
TALKING
ABOUT a shock
of blazing

TICKETS

Fun at the Weber County Fair

ROPE BORDER SCRAPBOOK PAGE

A softer version of the zigzag border is made with scalloped stripes.

YOU WILL NEED

- 2" x 12" (5.1 x 30.5 cm) strip of print paper (medium weight)
- 2" x 12" (5.1 x 30.5 cm) strip of coordinating print paper (medium weight)
- template #29, page 183
- tracing paper
- pencil
- scissors
- yarn

① Cut scallop shapes from the paper strips, using the template as a guide.

② Starting at the bottom wind the strips around each other to join.

① Cut the paper into twelve 2" x 8½" (5.1 x 21.6 cm) strips. Cut two 1" x 3½" (2.5 x 8.9 cm) strips from the scrap paper.

② Score the center length of the strips.

③ Fold each side in to the center.

④ Fold in half at the score line. Repeat with the remaining strips.

⑤ Fold the strips in half, crosswise.

⑥ Hook strips together at right angles.

⑦ Add two more strips.

⑧ Noting the weaving pattern used in step 7, weave two additional horizontal strips with the three vertical strips.

⑨ Weave together the remaining strips.

⑩ Place the coaster on the craft table and pull the ends to tighten the woven strips.

⑪ With the wrong side up, place one scrap rectangle along one raw edge.

⑫ Turn the coaster over and staple through all layers.

⑬ Place a narrow strip of double-sided adhesive on the wrong side of the rectangles, covering the staples.

⑭ Fold the scrap in half lengthwise over the adhesive.

⑮ Trim the strip ends.

⑯ Repeat steps 11 through 15 in the adjoining side.

OFFICE SCRAPS COASTER

Cut the clutter, save the environment, and protect your desktop all at the same time. Weave recycled office paper into coasters and you can multitask with a smile.

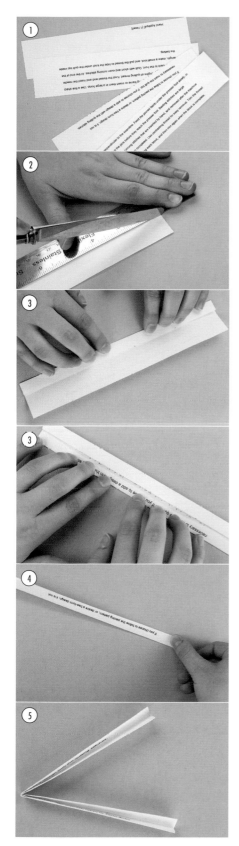

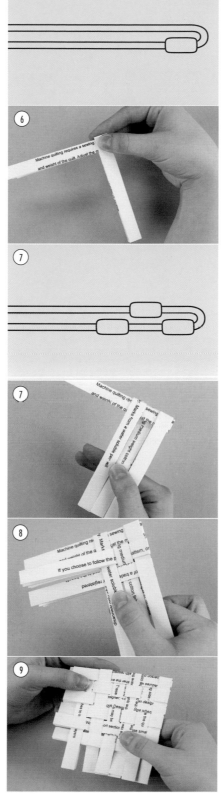

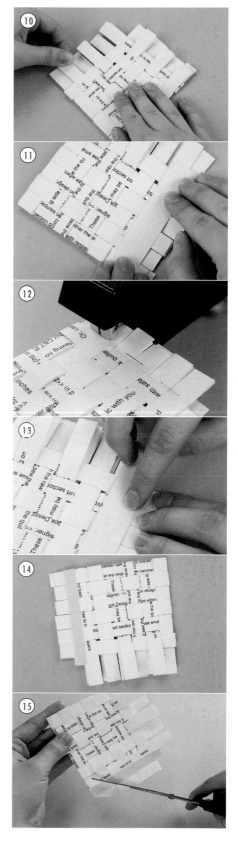

STITCHING ON PAPER

Put a needle and thread to work and create high-fashion paper pizzazz. Hand or machine stitches can be used to attach paper appliqués, to join strips, or to add textural details. Adopt a smart stitching strategy and you will look at paper in a whole new way. If you are a beginner, follow these simple guidelines and your success is almost guaranteed. If you are an experienced seamstress, substitute paper for fabric and think outside the sewing basket!

Hand Stitching

Decorate a page with a single French knot or an entire backdrop of cross-stitches. This age-old technique will dress up your projects and take you back to a time when embellishment was truly an art form.

Select rigid paper or card stock. Lightweight paper such as textweight paper will tear easily and is not stiff enough to remain flat during and after handling. Use embroidery floss, available at craft and needlework stores. Floss comes in a variety of colors and fibers. Because individual skeins are inexpensive, pick up a rainbow of colors.

Practice stitching on a paper scrap to achieve even stitching tension. Stitches that are worked loosely will not lie flat on the paper, and pulling too tightly will tear the paper. The projects in this chapter feature five basic embroidery stitches. They include a straight stitch, a cross-stitch, a running stitch, a backstitch, and a French knot.

Straight stitch, cross-stitch

Running stitch

Back stitch

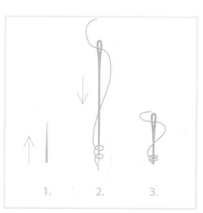

French knot

Hand stitching on paper

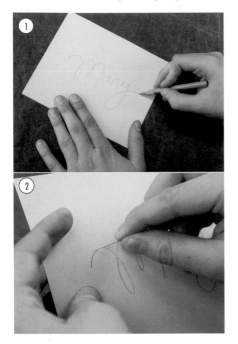

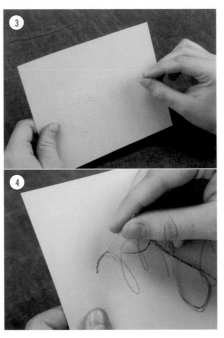

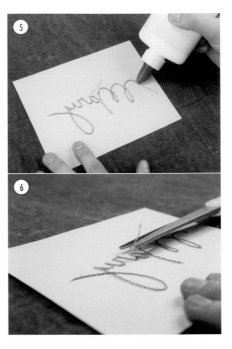

① Draw the design or script on the front of the paper. Choose a colored pencil that coordinates with the selected floss color. In order to hide the marked lines, you may choose to draw on the back of the paper. Keep in mind that images will need to be drawn in reverse.

② Use the straight pin to pierce holes in the paper along the marked line. Space the holes ⅛" to ¼" (3 to 6 mm) apart.

③ Cut a short length of floss, approximately 10" (25.4 cm). Short lengths are easier to draw through the pin holes and are less likely to twist or knot. Separate the strands and thread two strands in the needle. It is not necessary to knot the end of the floss strand. Because a knotted end may pull through the pinhole to the front of the paper, the end is secured with glue or tape after the stitching is complete. Insert the needle on the back of the paper and draw it through to the front. Leave at least 2" (5.1 cm) at the end of the floss strand and hold it in place as you sew.

④ Working from left to right, backstitch through the pinholes. Take care when inserting the needle in the holes to avoid tearing the paper. Even slight tears may make the stitched line appear uneven.

⑤ When the stitching is complete, place the paper on the craft table with the wrong side up. To secure the ends, apply small drops of glue or squares of tape at the points at which the stitches start and stop.

⑥ Allow the glue to dry and trim the floss ends.

Machine Stitching

A sewing machine can be used to add distinctive lines and textures to your paper projects. The process is quick and easy, and any size or style of machine will do the trick. Stitching on paper will dull your needle, so designate one machine needle for paper only. Change to a sharp needle before returning to stitching on fabric.

It is possible to use small or closely placed stitches if you back the paper with nonwoven interfacing. It will reinforce the paper and prevent it from tearing along the perforated stitching line. It is not necessary to use interfacing if you choose a long straight stitch or an open zigzag stitch.

Before stitching, make sure that there is enough thread on the spool and on the bobbin to finish the project. If you stop stitching to rethread the machine, it will be difficult to resume stitching at the same point on the paper. Restarting will require you to align the machine with the pierced holes.

Choose light- or mediumweight papers, and don't stitch through more than two mediumweight or three lightweight layers. Use a scrap of paper to experiment with stitch length and machine tension. Perfect tension will display the top and the bottom threads evenly.

The projects included in this chapter feature machine satin stitch, straight stitch, zigzag stitch, and free-form stitching.

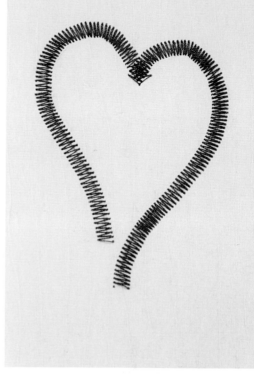

YOU WILL NEED

- tracing paper
- light- or mediumweight paper
- all-purpose sewing thread
- nonwoven interfacing
- pencil
- straight pin
- scissors

TIP

Nonwoven interfacing is recommended for satin stitch, and small straight stitch. Available at craft and fabric stores, this handy material is offered in a variety of weights. Light or medium weights work best for backing paper.

Machine free-form stitch

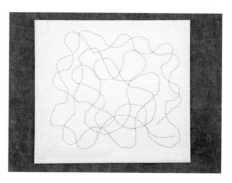

① Adjust the machine to a long straight stitch. It is not necessary to mark the design on the paper before stitching. Stitch slowly while turning the paper. Although the design is random, try to balance the scribbled stitching line within the desired area.

Machine satin stitch

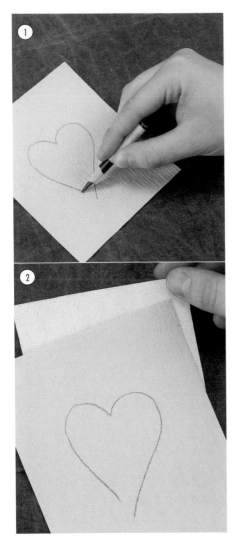

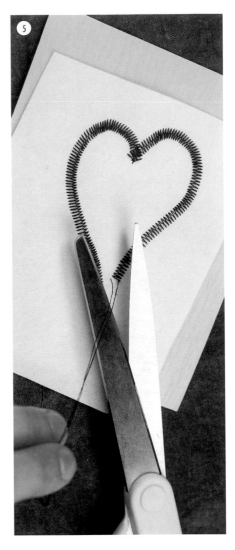

① Draw the design or script on the front of the paper. Choose a colored pencil that coordinates with the selected thread.

② Back the paper with a piece of interfacing that is larger than the marked image.

③ Adjust the machine to the desired settings. Stitch slowly and turn the paper and interfacing together to follow the marked line. When stitching a closed image, slightly overlap at the ends.

④ When the stitching is complete, place the paper on the work surface with the wrong side up. Pull the end of the bottom thread to create a loop in the top thread. Use the straight pin to bring the top thread to the back of the paper. Repeat with the second thread end.

⑤ Trim the excess interfacing from around the stitched image.

Machine straight and zigzag stitches

① Adjust the machine to the desired settings. Use both hands to guide the paper or papers through the machine.

② When stitching paper shapes, work slowly around the edges. When stitching a closed image, slightly overlap at the ends.

③ When the stitching is complete, place the paper on the work surface with the wrong side up. Pull the end of the bottom thread to create a loop in the top thread. Use the straight pin to bring the top thread to the back of the paper. Repeat with the second thread end. Glue or tape the thread ends.

Stitching Projects

EMBELLISHED GIFT TAGS

A few well-placed stitches dress up this trio of gift tags. Use preprinted tags or add old-world designs with rubber stamps.

Bird tag

Acorn tag

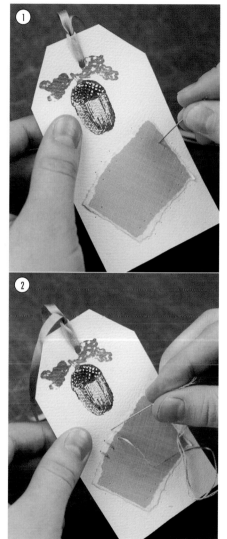

Cherries tag

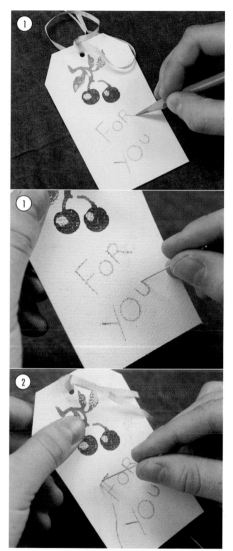

① Pierce holes. With dark orange floss, use a running stitch to outline the bottom of the tag.

② Pierce additional holes and add straight stitches and French knots.

③ On the back of the tag, apply small dots of glue to secure the floss ends. On the front, add a message strip with glue or double-sided adhesive.

① Tear a square of contrasting paper and place it on the tag. Pierce holes through both layers along the edge of the square. Then pierce corresponding holes on the tag.

② Stitch the square to the tag with the light orange floss.

③ Apply small dots of glue to secure the floss ends, and finish by writing a message on the tag.

① Use a pink pencil to address the tag, and pierce holes along the marked lines.

② Backstitch the words with matching pink floss.

③ On the back of the tag, apply small dots of glue to secure the floss ends.

WELCOME TO THE NEIGHBORHOOD GREETING CARD

Who wouldn't want to live in a place with rolling hills and pie-in-the-sky stitched flowers? Say hello to your new best friend with this creative card.

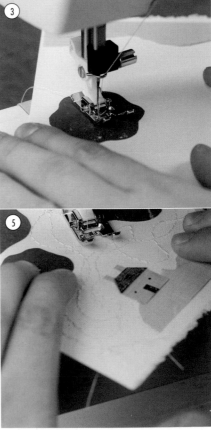

① Tear free form shapes from selected papers for the hills. Using template 30 on page 197, cut the house and the flower shapes.

② Arrange the hill and house shapes and attach them to the card with double-sided adhesive.

③ Adjust the machine to make a wide zigzag stitch. Place one flower on the front of the card and stitch slowly around the flower center. Because the flower center is small, rotate the card and flower after each stitch.

④ Repeat with the remaining flowers, and pull the thread ends to the back of the card.

⑤ Change the adjustment to make a long straight stitch, and make a free-form design in the negative space around the flowers.

⑥ Trim the thread ends and finish with a message strip that is attached with glue or double-sided adhesive.

BIRD NOTECARD

A duet of solid colors and simple shapes hits just the right note. Add a few stitches for a big finish on a small card.

① Using template 31, page 184 as a guide, cut the shapes from selected papers. Also cut a rectangle for the background.

② Attach the body, the wing, and the circles to the rectangle with double-sided adhesive.

③ Using the photo above as a guide, pierce holes for stitches. With coordinating floss, add straight stitches for detail.

④ Use navy floss to add French knots for the eyes, and back stitching for the legs.

⑤ Glue the feet in place.

⑥ Draw a beak with a dark colored pencil.

⑦ At the top of the card, make a single stitch, tie the ends into a knot, and trim.

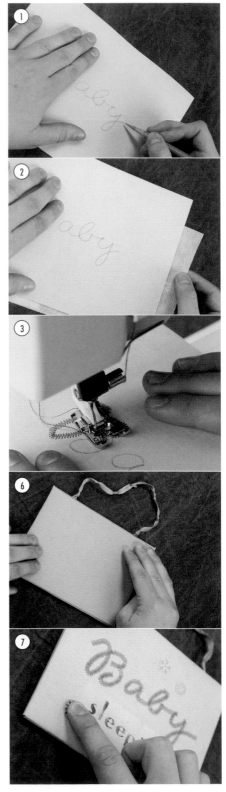

BABY SLEEPING SIGN

Make this miniature "Do Not Disturb" sign for your favorite baby. It's a stylish way to a good night's sleep.

① Use a lavender pencil to draw the message on the paper, using template 32 on page 184 as a guide.

② Place the paper on the interfacing.

③ Adjust the machine to make a narrow satin stitch and use coordinating thread to carefully stitch along the marked line.

④ From chipboard or cardboard, make matching rectangles.

⑤ Trim the excess interfacing and cover one rectangle with the stitched paper. Use contrasting paper to cover the second rectangle for the back of the sign.

⑥ With a ribbon handle sandwiched between them, glue the rectangles together.

⑦ Add stamped copy and accents with glue or double-sided adhesive.

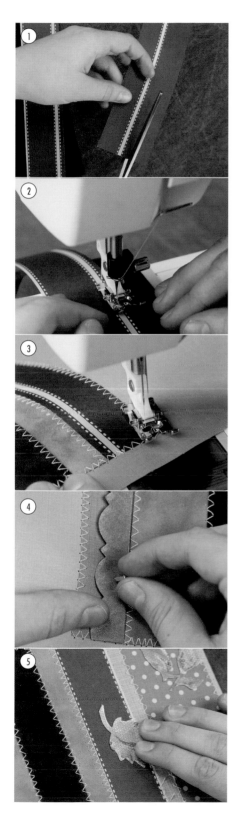

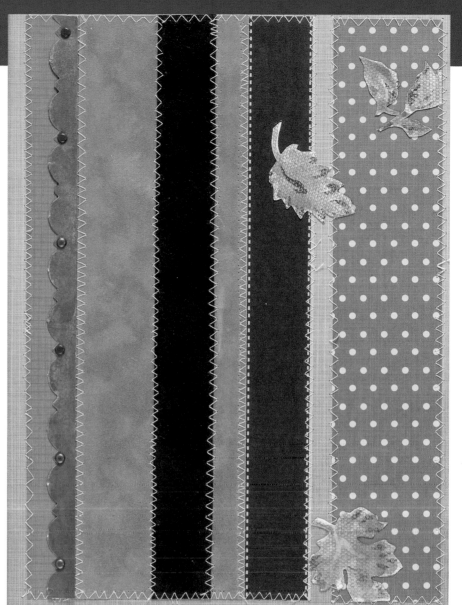

JOURNAL

If you need a handy place to pen your thoughts, don't give up art for utility.
Make this snappy stitched cover for a chipboard journal and stash it in
your travel bag or backpack.

(1) Cut strips of various widths from
selected papers.

(2) Choose contrasting thread. Slightly
overlap the long sides of the strips and
machine stitch them together with both
zigzag and straight stitches.

(3) Stitch the pieced sections to a larger
sheet of backing paper.

(4) Align a scalloped accent strip with a
stitched seam and attach it to the pieced
paper with brads.

(5) Cover the journal with the stitched
paper and add die cut accents with glue
or double-sided adhesive.

EDGY EDGED CARDS

Enchanting borders turn cards into
magic. No sleight of hand required,
just a few basic stitches.

Wrapped edge card

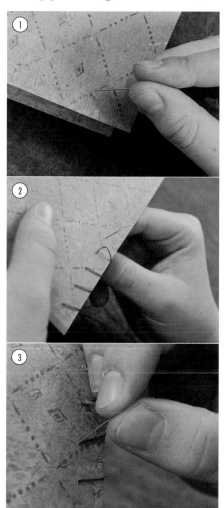

Cross-stitch card

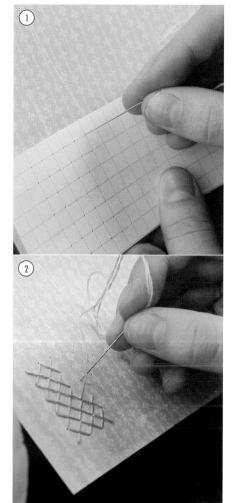

Sequined edge card

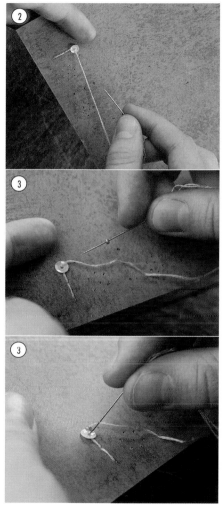

① Mark and pierce holes at ½"
(1.3 cm) increments.

② Working from left to right, wrap
mauve floss around the edge of the card.

③ Reverse direction, and return to the
first pinhole.

④ Adjust the stitches and on the back
side of the card, apply a long strip of
cellophane tape over the entire row.

① Trim a scrap of graph paper with a
¼" (6 mm) grid to the width of the card.
Align the paper along the bottom of the
card and pierce through both layers at
the intersections. Pierce the desired number of rows for stitching.

② Use variegated thread and working
from left to right, make cross-stitches.

③ Secure the ends with small dots of
craft glue or with cellophane tape.

① Refer to the photo on page 88, and
mark and pierce the edge of the card.

② With cream floss, use straight stitches
to make the stems and the spokes. Thread
a white sequin at the top of a stem.

③ Place a gold bead on the needle and
insert it in the same hole that was used to
secure the sequin.

④ On the back of the card, apply a
long strip of the cellophane tape over the
entire row.

PAPER CUTTING

Don't run with scissors! Instead find a comfy chair and settle in to make a paper-cut masterpiece. The technique is a study in contrasts, with projects that range from the simple to the sublime. Some are repetitive designs, made by cutting through layers of folded paper. Others are single designs that you cut through one layer with a craft knife. A few snips is all it takes to make charming retro paper dolls and snowflakes. And with a nod to German Scherrenschnitte, you can fashion an intricate heart or wreath.

Cutting Techniques

Choose a cutting method that suits your project. Some paper cutting is best done with a craft knife and cutting mat. Others are cut with scissors from paper that has been folded in one of the following ways:

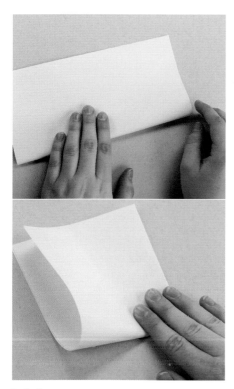

In halves or quarters

In thirds or sixths (triangles)

In an accordion pattern

Whether cutting with scissors or a knife, hold all of the layers securely to ensure accuracy. In order to make a cut tissue paper shape easier to handle and to glue in place, place it between two sheets of wax paper. Press with a warm iron to flatten and to infuse the tissue with wax.

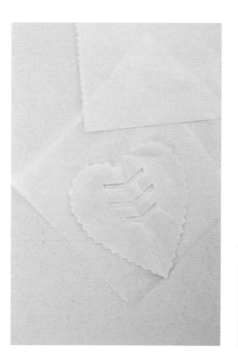

Paper Cutting Projects

PLACE MATS

Reveal traditional motifs with a handy craft knife. A bouquet, a butterfly, a fruit bowl, and a pair of doves make up this set of beautiful place mats. For easy cleaning, cover them with lightweight vinyl.

YOU WILL NEED

- mediumweight paper
- templates #33, 34, 35, 36, pages 185 to 188
- tracing paper
- double-sided adhesive
- pencil
- craft knife
- cutting mat
- oil cloth
- clear vinyl

(1) Transfer the designs to the mediumweight paper, using the templates as a guide.

(2) Use the craft knife to cut along the marked lines.

(3) Attach the top layer of paper to the bottom layer with double-sided adhesive.

(4) Sandwich the paper design between a rectangle of oil cloth and a rectangle of clear vinyl. Machine stitch around the outer edge.

a charmed life

ALPINE HEART

YOU WILL NEED

- square of pink tissue paper
- template #37, page 195
- wax paper
- tracing paper
- pencil
- scissors
- craft knife
- cutting mat
- iron

① Fold the tissue in half. Noting fold lines, transfer the design to the top layer, using the template as a guide.

② Cut through all layers. Use a pair of sharp scissors for the large areas and a craft knife for the small areas.

③ Unfold and press between two sheets of wax paper.

SNOWFLAKE GARLAND

Celebrate winter with a cheery draping of cut paper snowflakes and paper link chain. What a great way to entertain the kids on a school-is-closed snow day!

YOU WILL NEED

- 5", 6", 7", and 8" (12.7, 15.2, 17.8, and 20.3 cm) squares of lightweight paper

- templates #38, pages 191 to 193

- tracing paper

- pencil

- scissors

- craft knife

- cutting mat

① Fold each square into sixths. Noting fold lines, transfer the patterns to the top layers, using the templates as a guide.

② Cut through all layers. Use a pair of sharp scissors for the large areas and a craft knife for the small areas.

Greetings for Christmas
and the New Year

Mr. and Mrs. John Bleazard

Christmas Card from Grandpa - 1939

YOU WILL NEED

- 4" x 7" (10.2 x 17.8 cm) rectangle of wrapping paper

- 3" x 10¼" (7.6 x 26 cm) strip of wrapping paper

- templates #39, pages 191 and 195

- tracing paper

- pencil

- scissors

- craft knife

- cutting mat

1 For the flowers, fold the paper in a four-panel accordion pattern. For the houses, fold the paper in a six-panel accordion pattern. Noting fold lines, transfer the designs to the top layer, using the template as a guide.

2 Cut through all layers. Use a pair of sharp scissors for the large areas and a craft knife for the small areas.

SOUTH OF THE BORDER

Add a little Mexican flair to a greeting card
or scrapbook page with a shooting star or
Santa Fe heart motif.

YOU WILL NEED

- 6" (15.2 cm) square of tissue
  paper, turquoise or red
- template #40, page 189
- wax paper
- tracing
  paper
- pencil
- scissors

1 Fold the tissue into quarters. Noting
fold lines, transfer the design to the top
layer, using the template as a guide.

2 Cut through all layers. Use a pair of
sharp scissors for the large areas and a
craft knife for the small areas.

3 Unfold and press between two sheets
of wax paper.

HIGH NOON

YOU WILL NEED

- 8½" (21.6 cm) square of lightweight paper
- template #41, page 196
- tracing paper
- pencil
- scissors
- craft knife
- cutting mat

① Fold the paper in half. Noting fold lines, transfer the design to the top layer, using the template as a guide.

② Cut through all layers. Use a pair of sharp scissors for the large areas and a craft knife for the small areas.

BEEHIVE WREATH

YOU WILL NEED

- 6" x 7" (15.2 x 17.8 cm) rectangle of wrapping paper

- template #42, page 190

- tracing paper

- pencil

- scissors

- craft knife

- cutting mat

① Fold the paper into quarters. Noting fold lines, transfer the design to the top layer, using the template as a guide.

② Cut through all layers. Use a pair of sharp scissors for the large areas and a craft knife for the small areas.

SISTERS
EMILY AND
HANNAH
OVERTON
ARRIVING IN
AMERICA,
SPRING 1902

PAPER DOLLS

YOU WILL NEED

- 5" (12.7 cm) square of wrapping paper
- template #43, page 190
- scissors
- craft knife
- cutting mat

1 Fold the paper in a four-panel accordion pattern. Noting fold lines, transfer the design to the top layer, using the template as a guide.

2 Cut through all layers. Use a pair of sharp scissors for the large areas and a craft knife for the small areas.

DESERT FLOWERS

YOU WILL NEED

- 5" x 7" (12.7 x 17.8 cm) rectangle of blue tissue paper
- template #44, page 194
- wax paper
- tracing paper
- pencil
- scissors
- craft knife
- cutting mat
- iron

① Fold the tissue into sixths. Noting fold lines, transfer the design to the top layer, using the template as a guide.

② Cut through all layers. Use a pair of sharp scissors for the large areas and a craft knife for the small areas.

③ Unfold and press between two sheets of wax paper.

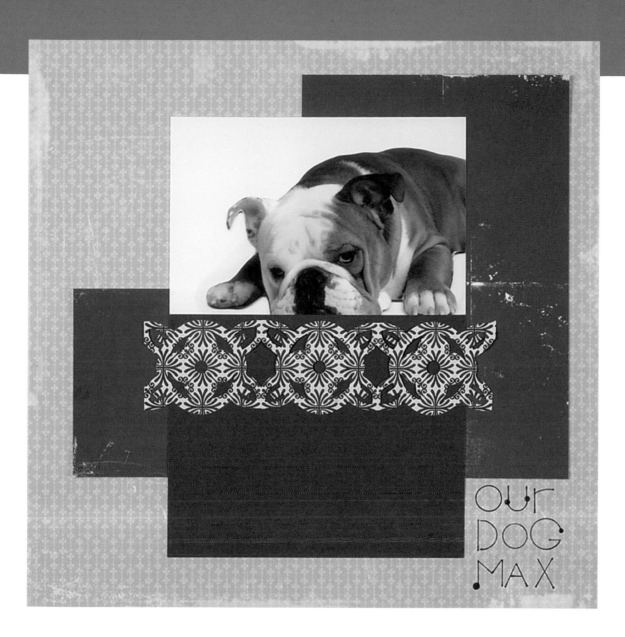

DON'T
FENCE
ME IN

YOU WILL NEED

- 2½" x 7" (6.4 x 17.8 cm) rectangle of wrapping paper

- template #45, page 194

- tracing paper

- pencil

- scissors

- craft knife

- cutting mat

(1) Fold the paper in a six-panel accordion pattern. Noting fold lines, transfer the design to the top layer, using the template as a guide.

(2) Cut through all layers. Use a pair of sharp scissors for the large areas and a craft knife for the small areas.

QUILLING

Women in colonial America amused themselves by making paper coils, and then using the coils to embellish paper samplers and hatboxes. The tools available to roll the coils were hat pins and quills, hence the name. This activity was held in such high esteem that most elite boarding schools taught "Quill Work" along with literature and music.

Quilling Techniques

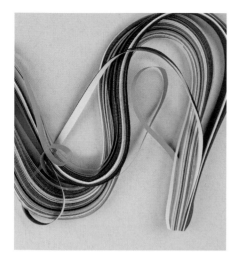

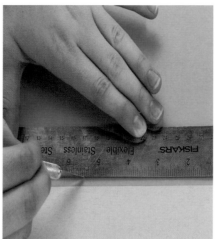

Precut quilling papers are available in ⅛" and ¼" (3 and 6 mm) widths.

To make your own, use a craft knife and a metal ruler to cut mediumweight paper into strips. For stiffer, looser coils, use construction paper strips.

A quilling tool is recommended to roll the strips. It is possible to shape the strips with your fingertips, but without a tool it is hard to achieve a uniform coil. And because the strips are narrow, hand rolling is more likely to crush them while shaping.

To make a coil

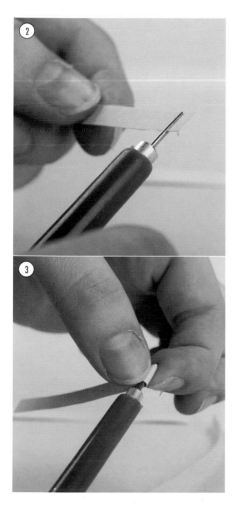

① Cut the strip to the desired length. Most models were made from short strips 3" to 4" (7.6 to 10.2 cm) long. For bigger shapes, cut longer lengths.

② Slide the end of the strip between the metal prongs of the quilling tool.

③ Keep the paper in place while rolling the tool handle.

④ Carefully remove the coil from the tool.

⑤ To secure the coils to a surface, squirt a shallow pool of white craft glue in a dish or on scrap paper. Pick up a coil with tweezers, dip the bottom in the glue, and place it on the surface.

Pinch and bend the coils to make additional shapes.

Square   Triangle   Ellipse   Leaf   Tombstone

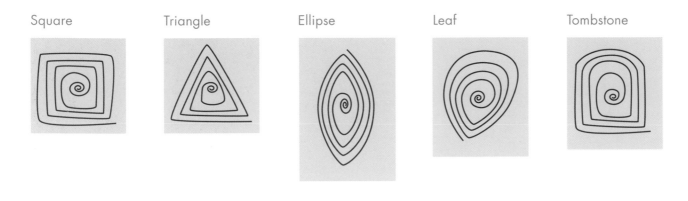

Combine shapes for mini three-dimensional images.

Fish

Flower

Boat

Person

House

Quilling Projects

QUILLED APPLIQUÉS

Quilled pieces glued to a base shape make adorable appliqués for paper crafting. Here, individual appliqués are featured on peek-a-boo note cards.

Heart appliqué

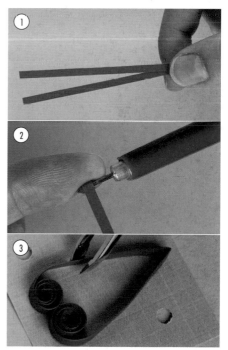

Lamb appliqué

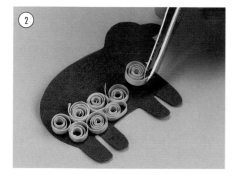

① Cut one lamb silhouette from the mediumweight paper, using the template as a guide.

② Make coils from 3" (7.6 cm) lengths of quilling paper. Glue the coils to the lamb shape. Let dry.

Leaf appliqué

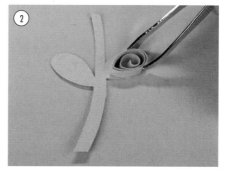

① Cut one leaf silhouette from the mediumweight paper, using the template as a guide.

② Make coils from 3" (7.6 cm) lengths of quilling paper. Pinch the coils to make tear drop shapes. Glue the coils to the leaf shape. Let dry.

① Cut a 6" (15.2 cm) length of quilling paper. Pinch at the center.

② Curl the ends to the center to form a heart shape.

③ Glue the heart to the backing paper.

FROSTED CUPCAKES

Scrumptious and calorie free! Make paper cupcakes with frilly quilled toppings to decorate for a party or commemorate a special birthday.

YOU WILL NEED

- template #47, page 175
- tracing paper
- paper cup with 2¼" (5.7 cm) base
- tissue papers in desired colors
- Styrofoam ball
- Paper Clay
- newspaper scraps
- wooden or wax candle
- papers: white quilling strips for the white frosted cupcake; orange medium-weight paper for the orange frosted cupcake; pink medium-weight paper for the pink frosted cupcake
- white craft glue
- scissors
- pencil
- quilling tool
- tweezers
- straight pins

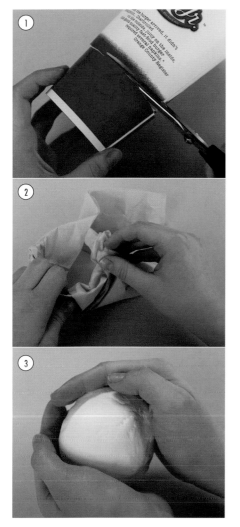

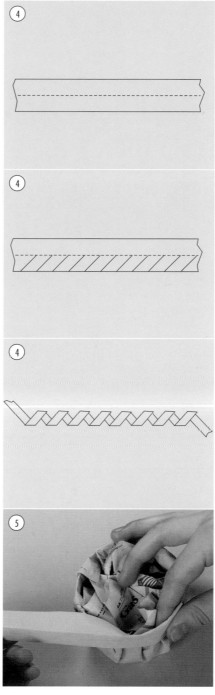

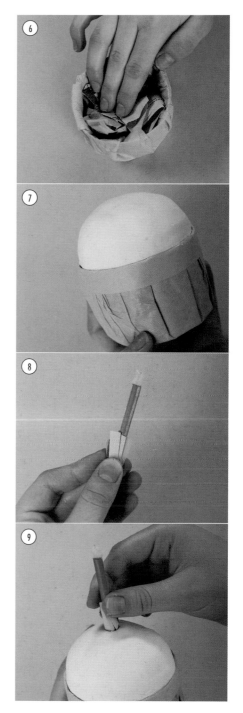

To make the cupcakes

① Cut a paper cup to the desired height. Choose a cup with a wide base.

② Cut large squares of tissue. Wrap the tissues around the base of the cup and tuck the edges inside.

③ Cover a foam ball with Paper Clay.

④ Cut a wide paper strip and fold it in half to make a flat band.

Or cut a narrow strip of paper and twist it diagonally to make a scallop band.

⑤ Cover the cup edge with the band.

⑥ Stuff newspaper scraps in the bottom of the cup.

⑦ Insert the ball in the cup.

⑧ Wrap short paper strips over the bottom of a wooden or wax candle.

⑨ Press the candle in the top of the cupcake. Let the cupcake dry.

White frosted cupcake

① Make coils from 3" (7.6 cm) strips.

② Glue the coils to the cupcake.

Orange frosted cupcake

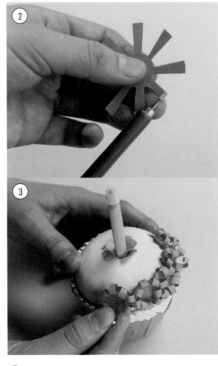

① Cut spoked shapes from the mediumweight paper, using the template as a guide.

② Coil the spokes of each shape.

③ Glue the coiled spokes to the cupcake. Hold the spokes in place with straight pins as the glue dries.

Pink frosted cupcake

① Cut 1¾" (4.5 cm) squares from the paper. Cut slits along opposite sides to within ¼" (6 mm) of the center.

② Coil the strips on each shape.

③ Glue the coiled strips to the cupcake. Hold the strips in place with straight pins as the glue dries.

LITTLE SPROUT

As if bald babies could be any cuter! A twist of quilled paper makes this one irresistible.

YOU WILL NEED

- artwork or photo of a baby
- two-tone paper
- cellophane tape
- quilling tool
- craft knife
- cutting mat

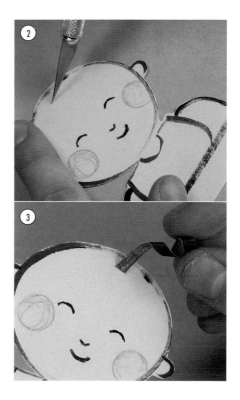

① Cut a ⅛" x 2" (3 mm x 5.1 cm) strip from the two-tone paper.

② Coil the paper with the quilling tool. Pull the end while releasing it to create a spiral.

③ Cut a slit in the artwork and slide the end of the spiral to the back. Tape in place.

GIFT BOW

Interesting things happen when you use your quilling tool to dress up a paper bow.

YOU WILL NEED

- lightweight colored paper
- scissors
- metal ruler
- quilling tool

① Cut a 1" (2.5 cm) strip from the full width of the paper. From the narrow ends, make cuts ⅛" (6 mm) apart to within 1" (2.5 cm) of the center.

② Wind a paper strip around the quilling tool. Pull the end while releasing it to create a spiral.

③ Curl the remaining strips.

④ Fold the rectangle in half, bring the curls together.

⑤ Fold in half again in the other direction.

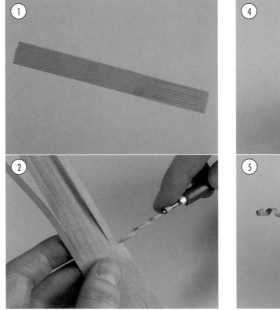

CARNIVAL MASK

A lovely quilled mask evokes a mood or provokes a memory.

YOU WILL NEED

- paper mask
- quilling paper
- white craft glue
- quilling tool
- tweezers

① Make coils from 3" (7.6 cm) strips.

② Glue the coils to the mask around each eyehole.

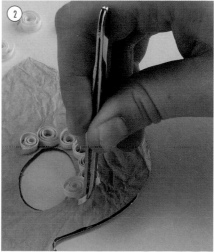

FRAME

Quill an edging around a mat window to give even simple artwork the royal treatment.

YOU WILL NEED

- light-weight paper
- frame
- metal ruler
- scissors
- quilling tool

① From the light-weight paper, cut two rectangles 2" (5.1 cm) wide and slightly longer than the width of the frame window. Cut two rectangles 2" (5.1 cm) wide and slightly longer than the length of the frame window.

② Refer to the diagram and cut slits in the rectangles.

③ Coil the strips.

④ Attach the strips to the frame.

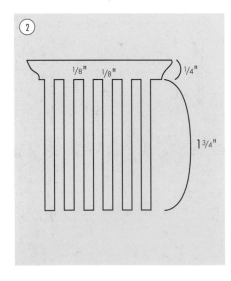

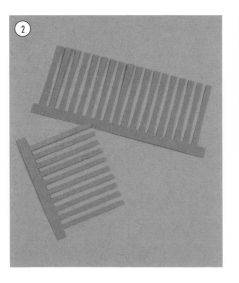

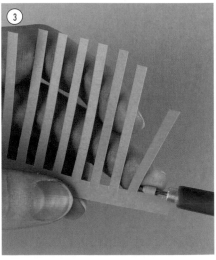

DELICATE ARC

An easy treatment makes ordinary paper seem special.

NAPKIN RING

A dainty quilled floral motif turns a simple paper napkin ring into a special memento.

YOU WILL NEED

- two-tone paper
- mediumweight paper
- templates #48, page 197
- tracing paper
- quilling paper
- pencil
- quilling tool
- hole punch
- adhesive
- tweezers

YOU WILL NEED

- quilling paper
- white craft glue
- quilling tool
- tweezers

① Make coils from 3" (7.6 cm) strips. Pinch them together at the ends to make disk shapes.

② Glue the shapes together in an arc shape.

① From the two-tone paper, cut one wave shape and one flower shape, using the templates as a guide.

② Cut and coil the quilling paper. Glue the coils to the flower. Let dry.

③ Punch a hole in the end of the wave. Tie some paper strips through the hole. Glue the flower to the end of the wave shape.

④ Bend and secure the loop at the slits.

JOURNALS

Wild enthusiasm for the scrapbook has boosted the image of its first cousin the journal. With an expanded definition, the word *journal* is now used as both a noun and a verb. With a small stack of paper and a little imagination, you can make a journal (noun) that is as personal as what you journal (verb).

Journal Details

The projects presented on pages 118 to 129 should be viewed as recipes for basic notebooks. Mix up your own versions by altering the sizes or the decorative elements. You can even customize the interior pages by adding tabs, a flap, a decorative corner, or a mini-envelope. If you are making a journal to present as a gift, consider making an ornamental bookmark or decorated pencil as an accessory.

Tab

 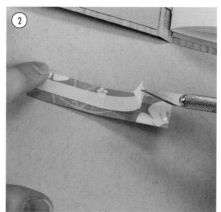 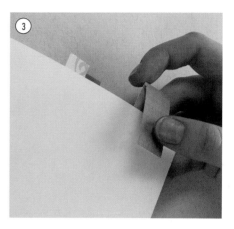

① Cut strips and fold in half.　　② Add double-sided adhesive.　　③ Attach to the top edge of the page.

Flap

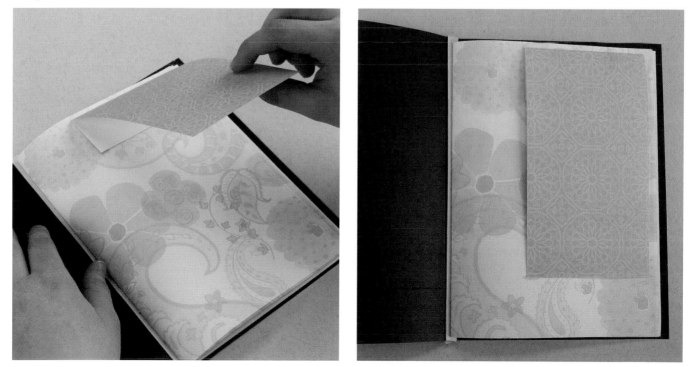

Fold down the edge of a rectangle, and attach it to the page with double-sided adhesive.

Corner

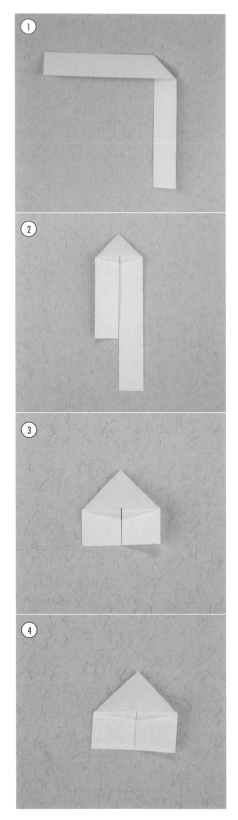

① Fold a strip at a right angle.

② Fold again to make a point.

③ Trim ends.

④ Add double-sided adhesive to the ends.

⑤ Attach to the page corner.

Bookmarks

Mini-envelope

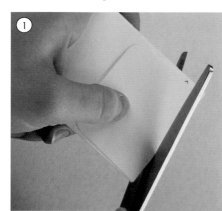

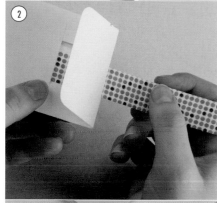

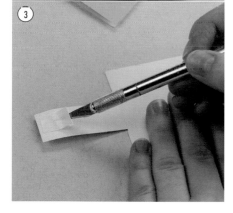

① Cut slits in the top and bottom edges of an envelope.

② Slide a strip of contrasting paper through the slits.

③ Attach double-sided adhesive to the ends.

④ Attach the strip to the page.

Pencil

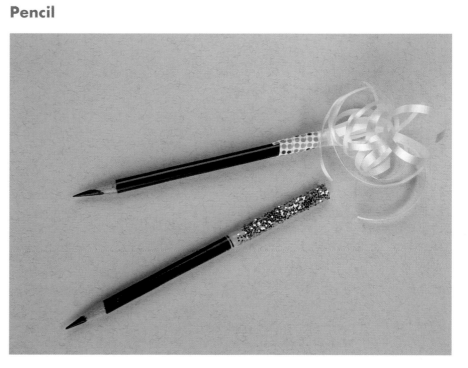

Journal Projects

WRAPPED TABLET

The jacket folded around this paper tablet will protect your important scribbles. Keep it nearby in case inspiration strikes.

YOU WILL NEED

- 8½" x 11" (21.6 x 27.9 cm) sheet of paper for the cover (heavy weight)
- desired number of 4½" x 7½" (11.4 x 19.1 cm) sheets of lightweight paper for the inside pages
- scoring tool
- paper punch
- ribbon
- metal ruler
- stapler

① Score the cover at the score lines indicated on the diagram.

② Fold the sides in along the scored lines.

③ Center the pages in the cover and staple along the top edge.

④ Center the pages a hole in the left flap and insert the ribbon.

⑤ Fold in the right and left flaps and wrap the ribbon around the cover. Tie in a knot.

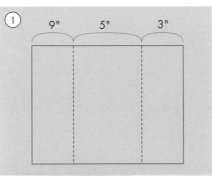

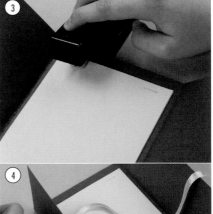

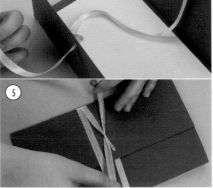

BUTTON BOOKLET

Who's got the button booklet?
Make a handful of these handy
notebooks and pass them around to
your circle of friends.

YOU WILL NEED

- two 4" x 5" (10.2 x 12.7 cm)
  sheets of paper for the cover
  (medium to heavy weight)
- desired number of 4" x 5" (10.2
  x 12.7 cm) sheets of paper for
  the inside pages (light-weight)
- two buttons
- thread
- decorative paper accents
- craft knife
- cutting mat
- needle
- scissors

① Mark the cover sheets at the dots
indicated on the diagram. Layer the
cover sheets and with the craft knife
pierce a hole through each at the dot.

② With the needle pierce a hole in one
page at the dot indicated on the diagram.
Repeat with the remaining pages.

③ Stack the pages between the covers.
Place a button on the pierced hole and
insert the needle through all layers.

④ Thread the needle through the
second button on the back of the cover.
Working from the back to the front,
thread the needle through all layers.

⑤ Repeat several times, knot the
thread, and trim the thread ends.

⑥ Embellish the cover as desired.

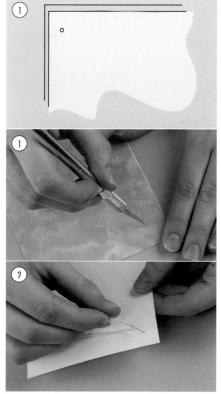

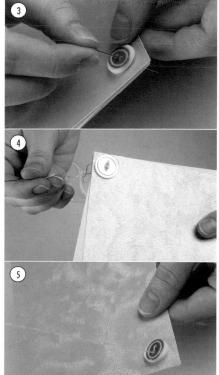

STITCHED JOURNAL

Based on traditional stitched books, this version joins the pages to a support strip with thread, then joins the strip to the cover with double-sided adhesive.

YOU WILL NEED

- 8¼" x 12" (21 x 30.5 cm) sheet of paper for the cover (medium to heavy weight)

- six to ten sheets of 8" x 11¼" (20.3 x 28.6 cm) paper for the inside pages (light weight)

- ³/₈" x 12" (1 x 30.5 cm) strip of chipboard (gift boxes are the perfect weight and density)

- thread

- double-sided adhesive

- metal ruler

- scoring tool

- pencil

- needle

- scissors

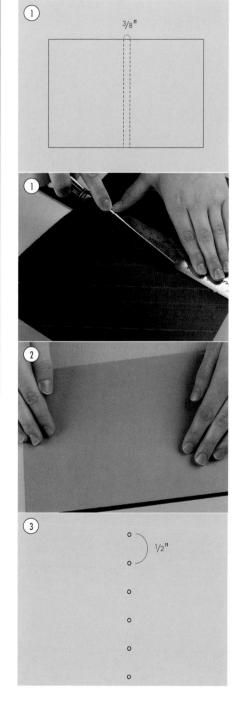

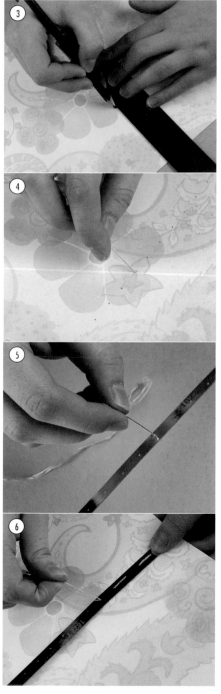

① Score the cover at the score lines indicated on the diagram.

② Fold the sides in at the score lines.

③ Mark the pages at the dots indicated on the diagram.

④ With the needle, pierce the pages at the marked dots.

⑤ Mark and pierce the strip at the dots indicated on the diagram.

⑥ Center the strip on the stacked pages and stitch through all layers. Knot and trim the thread ends.

7 Cut a narrow strip of double-sided adhesive and apply it to the chipboard strip. Remove the protective paper from the adhesive.

8 Open the cover on the craft table. Align the chipboard strip to the center of the cover and press in place.

9 Open the book at the center and place it right side up on the craft table. Cut narrow strips of double-sided adhesive and apply them to the ends of the chipboard strip. Remove the protective paper from the adhesive.

10 Bend the ends to the right side of the cover and press in place.

11 Embellish the cover as desired.

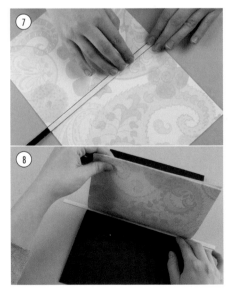

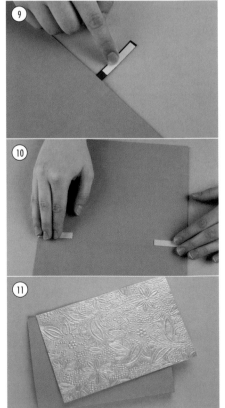

ACCORDION ALBUM

Record the ultimate run-on sentence in a book that expands with your imagination. When you are done writing, you can display your work on a dresser or tabletop.

YOU WILL NEED

- two sheets of 3¼" x 5¼" (8.3 x 13.3 cm) paper for the cover (heavy weight)
- four sheets of 3" x 12" (7.6 x 30.5 cm) paper for the inside pages (light to medium weight)
- rubber cement
- ribbon

① Fold each inside page in an accordion pattern as indicated on the diagram.

② To make one folded strip, refer to the diagram and glue the ends together with rubber cement.

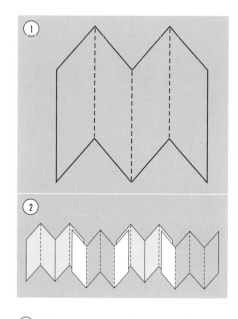

③ Glue one cover sheet to each strip end with rubber cement.

④ Wrap with ribbon to close.

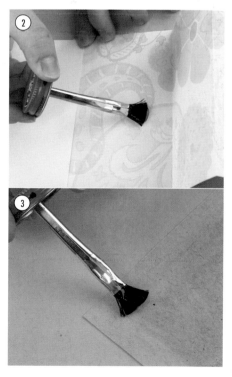

NOTEBOOK OF KNOTS

You can build this clever book in no time at all. Assemble the folded pages within the cover and then tie it all together in a bright red happy ending.

YOU WILL NEED

- 8½" x 11" (21.6 x 27.9 cm) sheet of paper for the cover (medium to heavy weight)
- desired number of 8" x 10¼" (20.3 x 26 cm) sheets of paper for the inside pages (light weight)
- yarn
- decorative paper accents
- metal ruler
- scoring tool
- pencil
- paper punch

1. Score the cover at the score lines indicated on the diagram.

2. Mark the cover at the dots indicated on the diagram.

3. Fold along one scored line, and punch through both layers at the marked dots.

4. Refold along the other scored line, and using the punched holes along the spine as a guide, punch through the remaining side.

5. Fold one sheet of lightweight paper in half.

6. Place the paper in the cover and fold. Using the punched holes along the spine as a guide, mark the paper.

7. Punch through both layers at the marked dots. Repeat with the remaining pages.

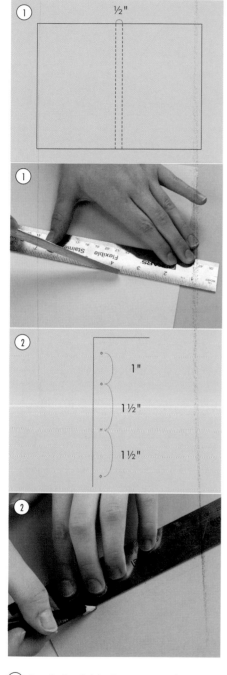

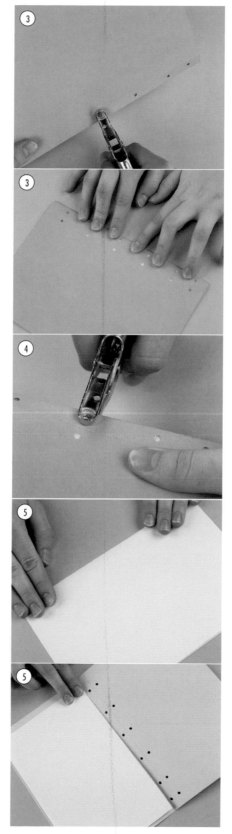

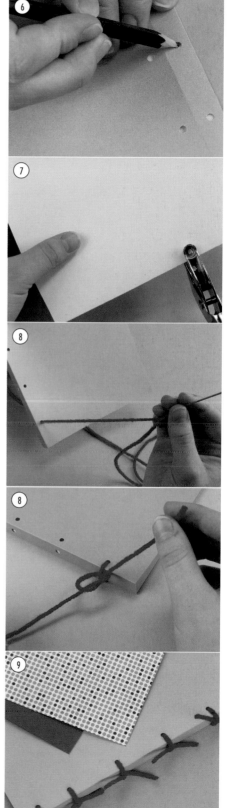

⑧ Stack the folded pages and insert them in the cover. Thread the yarn through the cover and the inside pages and tie the ends in a knot. Note that the holes punched along the spine are used only as a guide. Thread the yarn through the holes along the outside edges only.

⑨ Complete with the remaining holes and embellish the cover as desired.

DECO FOLIO

An eye-catching way to create a simple binding, the dowel adds stability
and decoration. A win-win for a winsome journal.

YOU WILL NEED

- two 5" x 8" (12.7 x 20.3 cm) sheets of paper for the cover (medium to heavy weight)
- desired number of 4¾" x 7¾" (12.1 x19.7 cm) sheets of paper for the inside pages (lightweight)
- 5" (12.7 cm) dowel
- decorative paper accents
- thread
- scoring tool
- metal ruler
- pencil
- needle
- scissors

(1) Score the cover sheets at the score lines indicated on the diagram.

(2) Mark the cover sheets at the dots indicated on the diagram.

(3) With the needle, pierce the cover sheets at the marked dots.

(4) Mark and pierce the inside pages at the marked dots.

(5) Stack the pages and layer them between the cover sheets. In an over/ under pattern, stitch through all layers. At the end of the seam, loop the thread again through all layers.

(6) Lash the dowel to the front cover. Use the same holes that were used to stitch the layers together.

(7) Knot the thread and trim the thread ends.

(8) Embellish the cover as desired.

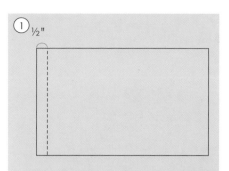

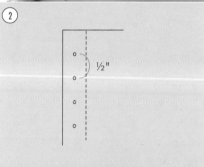
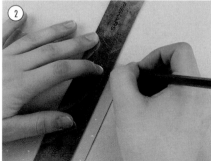

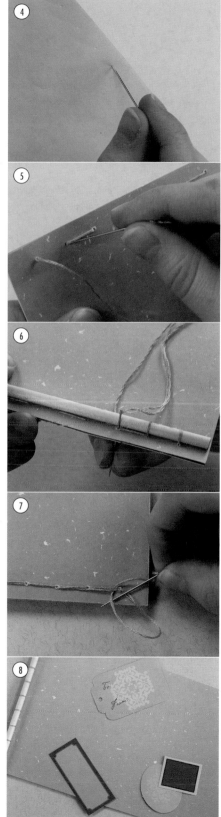

DECOUPAGE

The beauty of decoupage is in its simplicity: cut and paste. Three hundred years ago, wealthy Venetians employed master painters to decorate their walls and furniture. The idea trickled down to the masses and took the form of printed artwork that was cut from paper and glued in place. Thus was born the Italian label for this technique—*arte povera* or poor man's art. The Asian version features many layers of shiny lacquer applied to dark furniture. Modern adhesives that are specially formulated for decoupage make this craft fun and easy.

Surfaces and Papers

The best surfaces for decoupage are smooth and nonporous such as wood, metal, and plastic. When working on wood, sand and seal with paint or varnish before gluing the paper in place. If you use lightweight paper and a brush with soft bristles, it is possible to decorate surfaces with ridges, but avoid surfaces with bumps as they will tear or wrinkle the paper. Book covers can be used as a substrate but must be rigid enough to accept varnish without warping.

Choose decorative papers that are light to medium weight; heavy papers require more layers of varnish to blend the cut edge. Or try specialty papers designed for decoupage. They are made to look like paintings and are connected to a paper frame by small tabs. You can also use wrapping paper or novelty paper shapes. Additional paper options include images cut from books, magazines, and napkins.

Decoupage papers

Wrapping paper

Novelty paper shapes

Techniques

When cutting shapes from paper, you can alter the appearance by cutting around the image or leaving a contrasting border around the image. You can also layer papers to create borders.

Use adhesives that are formulated especially for decoupage, diluted white craft glue, or spray adhesive to apply the paper to the surface. Avoid using rubber cement, as it may leave raised brushstrokes. When layering papers, start with a lightweight paper such as tissue paper.

Add the second paper. Watch the edges as they dry, and press them back in place if they start to curl.

If you want a lustrous or durable finish, coat the surface with varnish. Choose from liquid or spray varnish. Follow the manufacturer's directions and apply a thin coat. Allow the varnish to dry completely and apply a second coat. Repeat until the desired veneer is achieved.

Decoupage Projects

VINEGAR BOTTLE BUD VASE

Some bottles are too good to toss. Size up your empties before you put them in the recycle bin.

HARLEQUIN ORNAMENTS

Stripes never seem to go out of style. Make these beautiful ornaments by decoupaging paper strips onto glass eggs. A sprinkling of fine iridescent glitter between coats gives them extra sparkle.

CD COASTERS

With a resin coating, these CDs serve as attractive coasters. Back them with cork or nonstick shelf liner.

FRAME

Botanical illustrations were cut from an old picture book to decorate this very old frame.

HATBOX

With abundant embellishments you can turn a cardboard hatbox into a fashionable hiding place for ribbons, sewing notions, or your favorite accessories.

EGG

Paper stickers transform a craft-store wooden egg into an old world treasure.

PITCHER PERFECT

Timeworn enamelware takes on new life with a simple decoupage decal.

CLOCK

What time is it? Time to loosen up your tie.

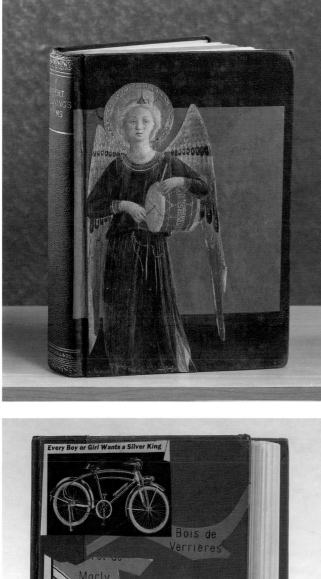

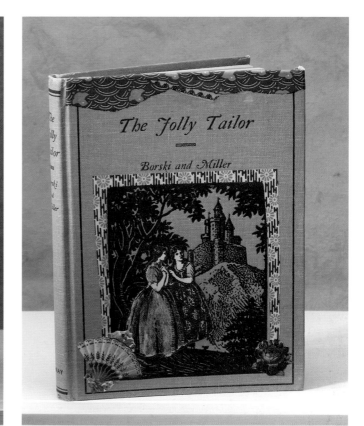

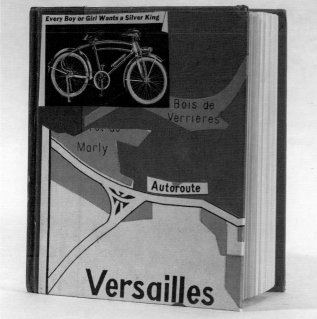

From the best-seller list to the best-dressed list, these books make the grade.

SCULPTING

Mild-mannered paper lying flat on your craft table is actually the stuff of dynamic sculpting. In the blink of an eye it can be transformed into super home decor projects, clever gift embellishments, or whimsical ornaments. This is an area of paper crafting where two-tone paper or paper that is printed on both sides can really make an impact. Try your hand at some of these projects or experiment with cutting and folding to sculpt original designs. Table toppers, tree toppers, cake toppers... these sculpting projects are all tops!

Sculpting Projects

Projects require paper that is weighty enough to hold its shape without drooping.

SALTWATER SANDALS

These paper sandals are sure to warm the heart of anyone who has strolled along a sunny beach.

① Cut the sole and the band shapes, using the templates as a guide.

② Reverse the patterns and cut a second set of shapes.

③ With the craft knife, pierce holes in the shapes where indicated. Cut slits in the bands where indicated.

YOU WILL NEED

- two 12" x 12" (30.5 x 30.5 cm) sheets of two-toned scrapbook paper (medium to heavy weight)
- templates #49, page 198
- tracing paper
- double-sided adhesive
- four small brads
- pencil
- scissors
- craft knife
- cutting mat

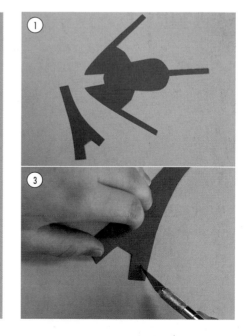

④ Cut small squares of double-sided adhesive and attach them to the wrong sides of the shapes as shown.

⑤ Fold the side flaps up along the dotted lines.

⑥ Slide and attach the flaps to the bottom of the sole.

⑦ Insert and secure a brad through the pierced holes.

⑧ Fold the band ends under along the dotted lines.

⑨ Align the pierced holes of the sole and the band end, and insert and secure a brad.

⑩ Attach the remaining ends to the bottom of the sole.

⑪ Slide the toe strap through the slits.

⑫ Tie a loose knot with the strap ends and pinch to secure.

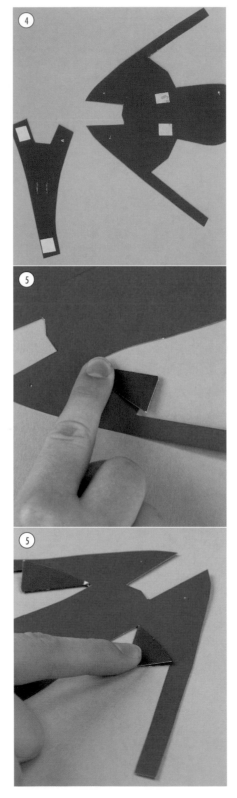

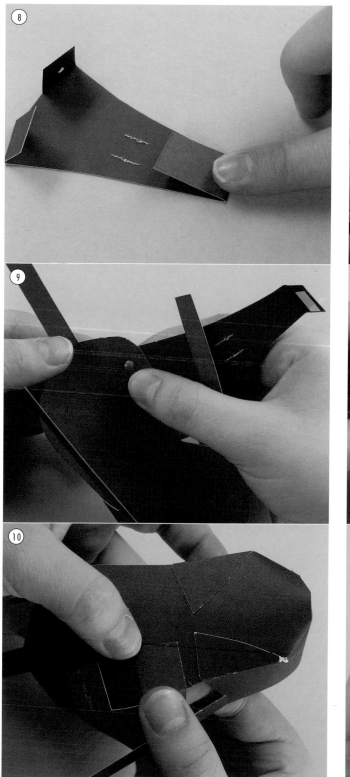

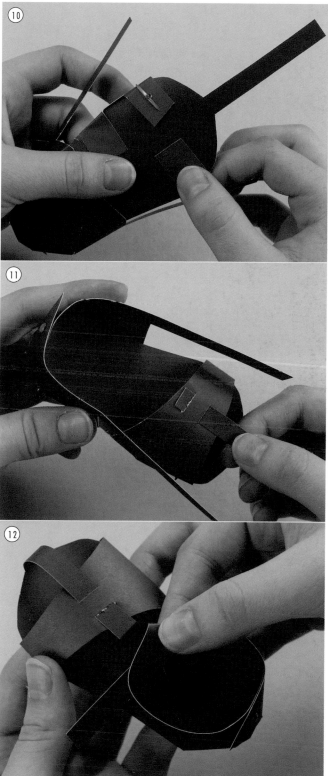

GUARDIAN ANGEL

Options for Angel's skirt are endless. Perch her on a bedpost or bookshelf where she can keep an eye on things.

YOU WILL NEED

- 12" x 12" (30.5 x 30.5 cm) sheet of scrapbook paper (medium weight)
- scrap of white scrapbook paper
- templates #50, page 199
- tracing paper
- double-sided adhesive
- pencil
- scissors
- stapler
- colored pencils

① Using the template as a guide, cut one angel shape from the scrapbook paper and one face from the white paper.

② Fold the notched edges up along the dotted line.

③ Bend the sides to the back and overlap the edges.

④ Staple the edges together.

⑤ Fold the neck flap down.

⑥ Highlight the face details with the colored pencils.

⑦ Apply a small square of double-sided adhesive to the back of the face and attach it to the neck.

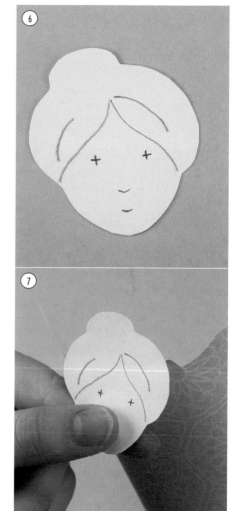

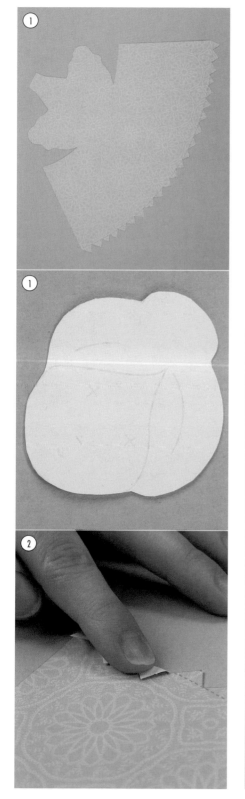

BUD VASE

Need an instant bud vase? In this perky paper disguise, even an empty pill bottle fills the role.

YOU WILL NEED

- 12" x 12" (30.5 x 30.5 cm) sheet of scrapbook paper (medium weight)
- metal ruler
- scissors
- pencil
- craft knife
- cutting mat

① Cut one 3" x 12" (7.6 x 30.5 cm) rectangle, and one 5" x 12" (12.7 x 30.5 cm) rectangle.

② Accordion-fold the narrow rectangle in four sections.

③ Mark an X in the center of the top fold. Mark a second X diagonal to the first.

④ Use the craft knife to cut along the marked lines through all layers.

⑤ Push up all of the cut triangles.

⑥ Starting from one short side, roll the large rectangle to form a tube.

⑦ Slide the cut section over the tube.

⑧ To balance the tube, adjust the folded sections at even angles.

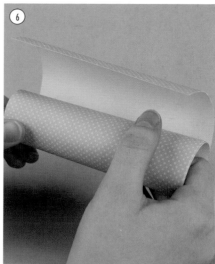

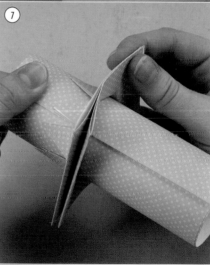

MAY BASKET

Fill this rectangular basket with candy sticks, pretzel rods, and lollipops. Then ring the doorbell and run!

YOU WILL NEED

- 12" x 12" (30.5 x 30.5 cm) sheet of scrapbook paper (medium to heavy weight)
- template #51, page 200
- tracing paper
- pencil
- scissors
- scoring tool
- metal ruler
- stapler

① Cut one basket shape, using the template as a guide.

② Cut slits in the shape where indicated.

③ Score along the dotted lines.

④ Fold the sides and ends in along the scored lines.

⑤ Place the basket shape on the craft table. Fold one end up and wrap the adjacent corners around it.

⑥ Staple through all layers. Repeat with the opposite end.

⑦ Fold the point of one end down. Repeat with the opposite end.

⑧ Staple the handles together at the pointed ends.

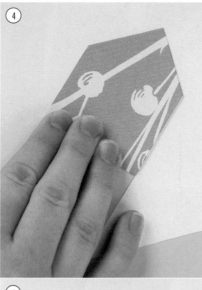

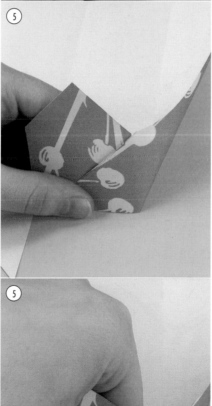

PINWHEEL

For a new spin on things, adorn a gift bag or box with a breezy pinwheel instead of a bow.

YOU WILL NEED

- 5½" (14 cm) square of two-toned paper (medium to heavy weight)
- small brad
- scissors
- craft knife
- cutting mat

① Pierce a small hole in the center of the square and cut slits from each corner to within ¼" (6 mm) of the center hole.

② In each of the triangles that have formed, pierce a hole in the bottom left corner, as shown.

③ Align one corner hole with the center hole.

④ Working clockwise, align the remaining holes with the center hole.

⑤ Insert the brad through all layers and secure.

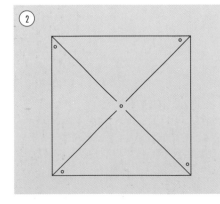

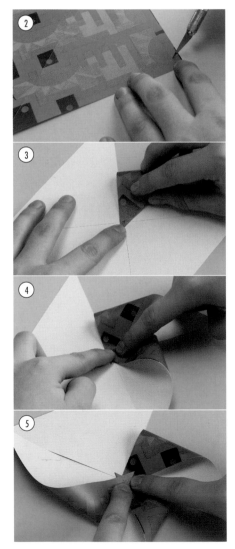

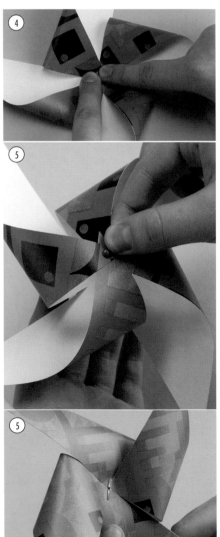

BOW

Ribbon's not the only way to pop extra panache on a gift box.

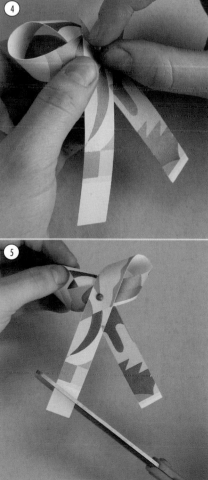

YOU WILL NEED

- ³⁄₈" x 12" (1.6 x 30.5 cm) strip of two-toned paper (medium to heavy weight)
- small brad
- craft knife
- cutting mat
- scissors

① With the wrong side up, make a loop in the paper.

② Make a second loop in the mirror image of the first.

③ Pierce the center through all layers with the craft knife.

④ Insert and secure the brad.

⑤ Trim the bow ends.

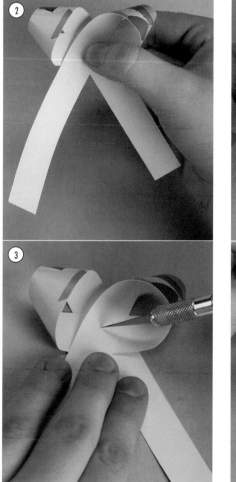

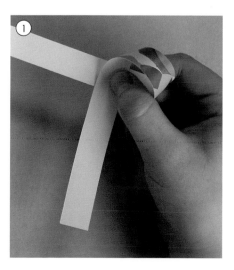

FAUX EASTER BASKET

All the best-dressed eggs are wearing them this season.

① Cut one basket shape, using the template as a guide. Cut one 3¾" x 9" (9.5 x 23 cm) rectangle from the coordinating paper. Cut ³⁄₈" x 2" (3 mm x 5.1 cm) slits along the long edge.

② Fold up the opposite long edge 1" (2.5 cm).

③ Slide the bottom of the basket shape between the cut edge and the folded edge.

④ Bend both shapes to make a cylinder and overlap the ends inside the fold.

⑤ Staple through all layers.

⑥ Bend the short ends down and tuck them behind the coordinating band.

⑦ Snip perpendicular slits in the handle ends.

⑧ Join the slits to secure the handle ends.

⑨ Crinkle the cut slits to resemble grass.

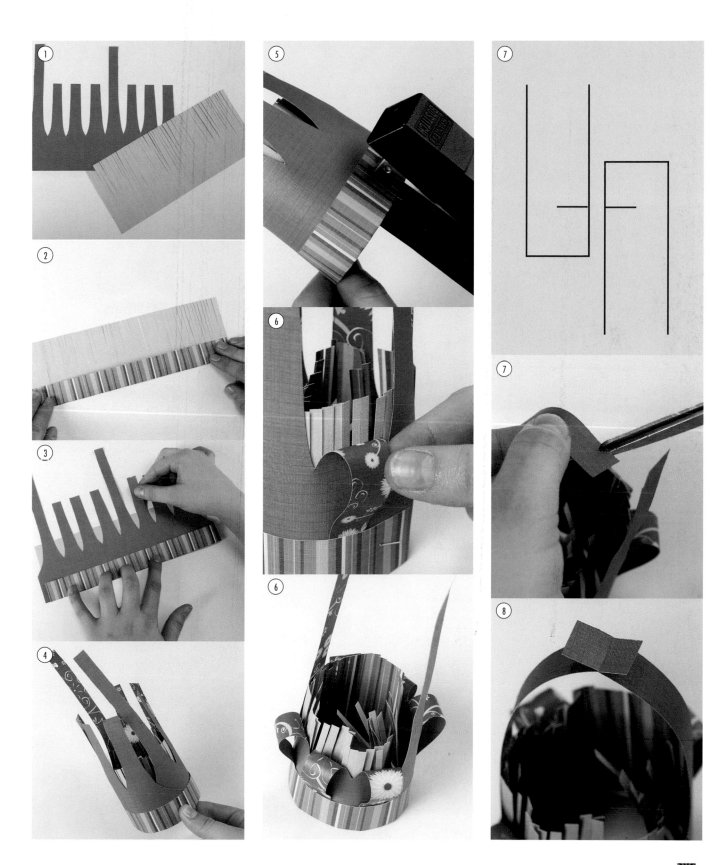

PAPIER-MÂCHÉ

Papier-mâché has long been the medium that allows artists to create lighter-than-air make-believe. From theatrical props to costume jewelry, you can build almost anything with this combination of paper and glue. And although they are light-weight, finished projects are sturdy enough to be carved and sanded. Ancient papier-mâché helmets have been unearthed in China that were strong enough to protect warriors from arrows and spears.

Simple Formula

The two ingredients required for papier-mâché are paper and paste.

Old newspaper is used most often because it is lightweight, porous, and easy to tear. And most of all because it is inexpensive and abundant. A wide variety of glue recipes can be used, some that include such exotic ingredients as bitter cucumber (to scrub the paper fibers), garlic (to repel insects), and cinnamon (to mask the smell of the garlic).

This recipe includes only four basic ingredients: flour, water, salt, and craft glue. You can use the white or wheat flour that is on your pantry shelf. If you desire stronger paste, use potato flour, and for smoother paste, use tapioca flour.

① In a saucepan, sprinkle ¼ cup flour into 2 cups of cold water and stir with a whisk. Place on low to medium heat and continue stirring as the mixture thickens. Cook until it becomes the consistency of runny mashed potatoes. If necessary, sprinkle in more flour and continue stirring. Remove any large lumps with a slotted spoon.

② Remove from the heat and let the paste cool. It will thicken slightly.

③ Add 1 teaspoon salt to prevent mold.

④ Stir in 3 to 4 tablespoons of white glue. This will make the paste smoother to work with and stronger when dry.

⑤ Tear the paper into small strips. Torn edges will blend better than cut edges.

⑥ Soak the strips in the paste.

⑦ Skim the excess paste from strips before applying them to the surface.

Allow the paste to dry completely between layers.

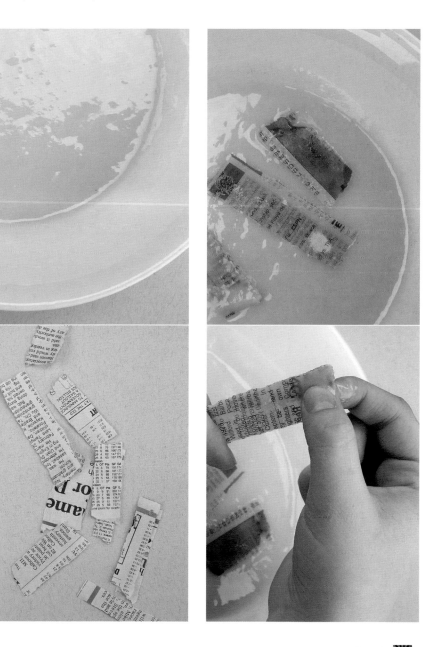

Papier-Mâché Projects

The models included in this chapter can be divided into two categories. Most projects have a framework or substrate under the papier-mâché. The papier-mâché is used as a finishing layer and/or to add texture. The vase and the party favors are in a different category. They take on the shape of their supporting forms, and when the forms are removed, the papier-mâché is self-supporting. These projects' integral strength is achieved with more layers of paper and paste.

APPLE TRAY

The ultimate green project: a multi-use tray made from materials resurrected from the recycle bin.

① Cut one cardboard tray shape and two handle shapes, using the templates as a guide.

② Score along the fold lines as indicated.

③ Fold up the sides and secure them with masking tape. Bend the handles down and glue the handle shapes on top.

④ Apply two to three layers of papier-mâché. Let dry.

⑤ Paint as desired.

YOU WILL NEED

- cardboard
- templates #53, page 202
- tracing paper
- masking tape
- white craft glue
- papier-mâché paste
- paintbrush or sponge
- newspaper
- paint
- scissors
- pencil
- metal ruler
- scoring tool

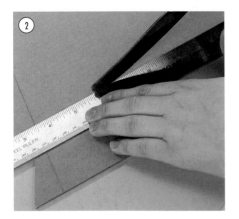

FLORAL FRAME

A favorite photo deserves a special setting.

YOU WILL NEED

- templates #54, pages 203 and 204
- tracing paper
- cardboard
- masking tape
- white craft glue
- papier-mâché paste
- newspaper
- paint
- pencil
- paintbrush or sponge

① Cut the cardboard frame and the appliqué shapes, using the templates as a guide.

② Glue the shapes to the frame.

③ Apply two to three layers of papier-mâché. Let dry.

④ Paint as desired.

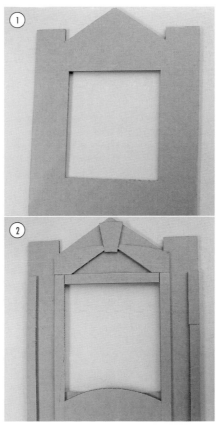

PEPPERMINT ORNAMENT

Fashion this ornament completely from scratch, or start with a cardboard ball from the craft store.

YOU WILL NEED

- newspaper
- masking tape
- tissue paper
- papier-mâché paste
- Paper Clay
- paint
- decorative accents
- paintbrush or sponge

① Form the newspaper into a ball and secure it with masking tape.

② Dip a sheet of tissue paper into the paste and wrap it around the ball. Smooth out any wrinkles and let dry.

③ Shape Paper Clay around the ball and let dry.

④ Paint as desired.

CARROT

Not the edible kind, but here's a carrot any bunny would be proud to call friend.

YOU WILL NEED

- newsprint
- template #55, page 205
- tracing paper
- pencil
- masking tape
- tissue paper
- papier-mâché paste
- paint
- decorative accents
- scissors
- pencil
- paintbrush or sponge

① Cut a fan shape from the newsprint, using the template as a guide.

② Roll the fan into a cone shape and tape the edge to secure. Stuff the cone with tissue paper.

③ Fold the top edge down and tape.

④ Apply two layers of papier-mâché. Let dry.

⑤ Paint as desired.

⑥ Add decorative accents.

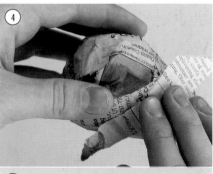

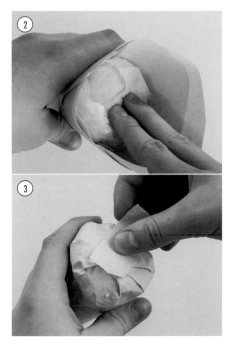

BALLOON BOWL

Make a bowl in any size by molding papier-mâché over a balloon.

YOU WILL NEED

- balloon
- papier-mâché paste
- newspaper
- recycled metal lid
- paint
- paintbrush or sponge
- scissors (optional)

① Blow up a balloon and cover the bottom with a layer of papier-mâché. Let dry.

② Apply two to three more layers of papier-mâché.

③ Pop the balloon and remove it from the form.

④ For an organic edge, leave it as. For a finished edge, trim it with scissors.

⑤ Place the metal lid on the bottom of the bowl. Apply two to three layers of papier-mâché to cover the lid. Let dry.

⑥ Paint as desired.

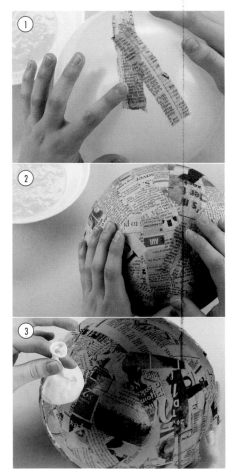

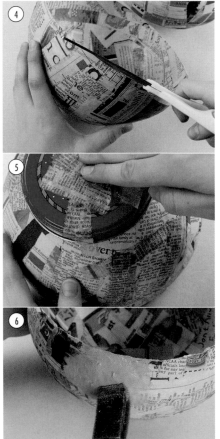

PARTY FAVOR CUPS

Spark the table conversation with readable party favors. Leave the newspaper unpainted.

YOU WILL NEED

- plastic drinking cup
- papier-mâché paste
- newspaper
- mediumweight paper
- double-sided adhesive
- decorative accents
- scissors

(1) Apply two to three layers of papier-mâché to the bottom of the cup. Let dry.

(2) Bend the plastic cup to remove the papier-mâché cup.

(3) Trim the edge.

(4) Cut strips of mediumweight paper and fold lengthwise. Cut perpendicular slits along one side.

(5) Attach the strips to the cups with narrow strips of double-sided adhesive.

(6) Decorate as desired.

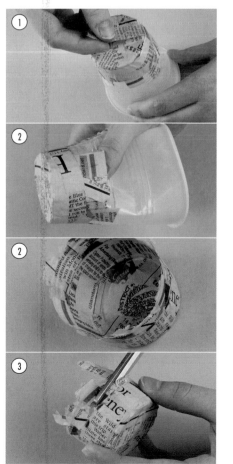

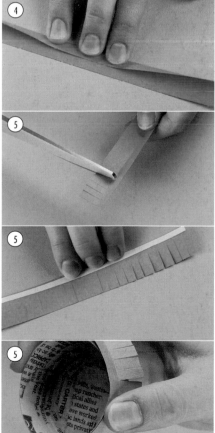

PRETZEL ORNAMENT

No-carb diet? No problem!

YOU WILL NEED

- balloon
- papier-mâché paste
- newspaper
- recycled metal lid
- paint
- paintbrush or sponge
- scissors (optional)

① Soak newspaper strips in the paste and wrap them around the cord in spirals.

② Place the cord on the wax paper and form it into a pretzel shape. Let dry.

③ Trim the ends and paint.

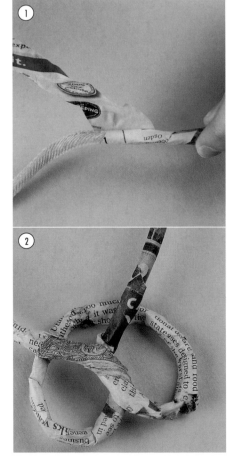

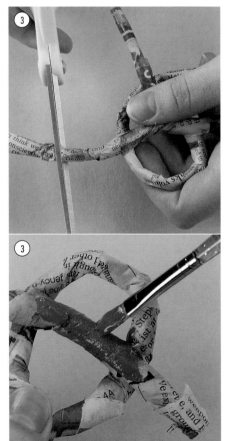

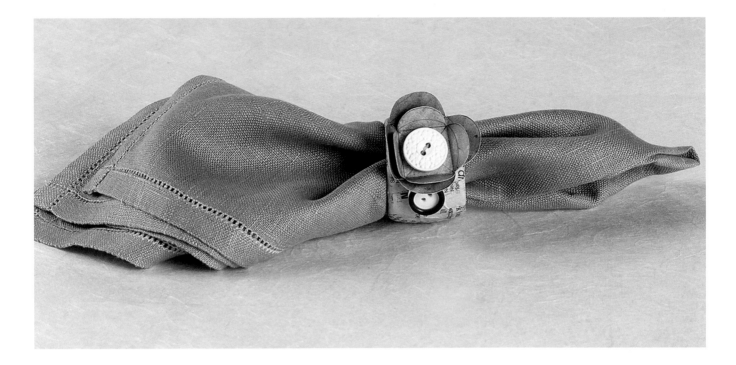

NAPKIN RINGS

For the uber inventive hostess.

YOU WILL NEED

- corrugated paper
- masking tape
- papier-mâché paste
- newspaper
- decorative accents
- scissors

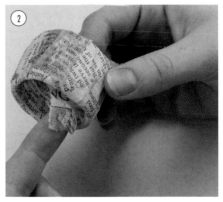

① Cut a strip of corrugated paper. Bend and tape it to make a ring.

② Apply two to three coats of papier-mâché. Let dry

③ Decorate as desired.

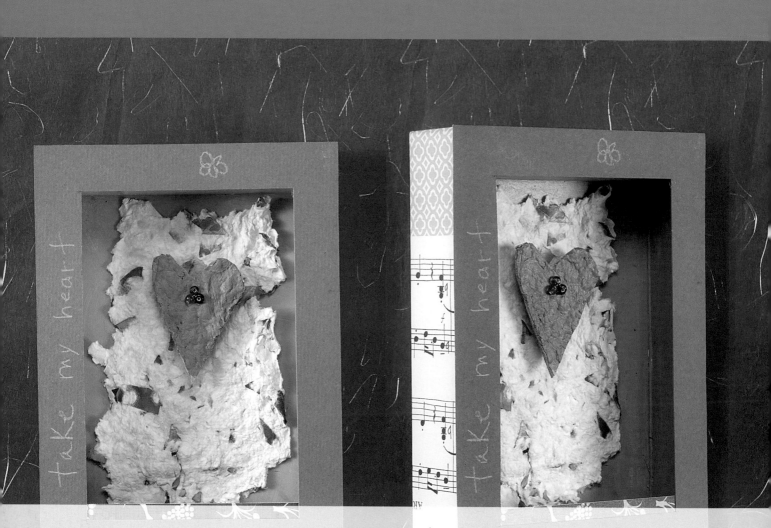

BLENDED AND MOLDED PAPER

When you really crave that hand-made look, make your own paper, either flat sheets or hand-molded shapes. The methods in this chapter are comparable to papier-mâché, but for both blending and molding, the shredded paper is further reduced to deconstructed pulp. Paper and fiber scraps are pureed to pulp in a household blender, poured onto a screen to remove excess water, and allowed to dry into unique paper sheets. Pulp combined with glue forms paper "dough" that can be molded into interesting shapes, dried, and painted. Let's get messy!

Blended Paper

Blended paper requires a household blender to whip the paper pulp together with air and water. After drying, the paper is somewhat fragile—it will break when bent and dissolve when wet.

YOU WILL NEED

- paper
- water
- non-flavored gelatin (optional)
- liquid starch (optional)
- blender
- screen (non-metallic screen stretched on a wooden frame)
- deckle (open frame that fits within the screen framework)
- paper towels

Screen

Deckle

Making blended paper

(1) Tear an assortment of lightweight papers such as computer, construction, and watercolor papers into small bits, (approximately 1" to 1½" [2.5 x 3.8 cm] squares), and drop them in the blender. Fill the blender with the paper to between ¼ and ½ capacity.

(2) Pour 1 cup of hot water on the paper and let it sit for 15 minutes. Then pour in enough water to cover the paper.

(3) Blend by turning the pulse knob on and off until the paper is pulverized and blended evenly with the water.*

(4) Place the deckle on the screen and hold them level over the sink. Pour in the mixture and let it drain through the screen.

(5) Remove the deckle.

(6) To accelerate drying, blot the pulp with paper towels.

(7) Allow the paper to air-dry.

*If you want to be able to write on the dried pulp, add unflavored gelatin to blended paper and pulse a final time. This will seal the fibers. If you want to make the dried pulp stronger, add two to three tablespoons of liquid starch to the blended paper and pulse a final time.

Blended Paper Projects

LIGHTER-THAN-AIR BEAR

Shallow molds made for candy or clay can also work for blended paper. With a nod to chocolatiers, make a molded bear that will last through the holidays and beyond.

YOU WILL NEED

- blended pulp made from white lightweight paper, green mediumweight paper, and orange mediumweight paper
- nonstick cooking spray*
- acrylic paint (optional)
- frame
- white craft glue
- paper accents
- mold
- scissors (optional)
- paintbrush (optional)

① Press drained pulp into the treated mold. Slightly mound the pulp above the edge of the mold, as the shaped mass will shrink as it dries.

② Allow the pulp to dry.

③ Carefully remove the shape from the mold.

④ Trim the excess paper from the edges, if desired.

⑤ Highlight the details with the paint. Note that the shaped mass will dissolve when wet, so limit paint to small areas.

⑥ Attach the bear to the back of the frame with white craft glue. Decorate the frame with the paper accents.

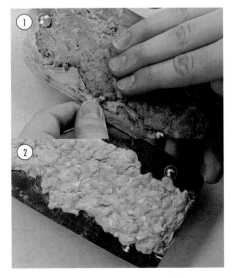

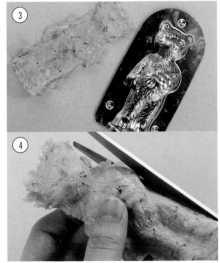

*If the mold is not coated with a nonstick surface such as Teflon, it is necessary to spray the inside of the mold with nonstick cooking spray to allow for easy release.

LOOSE ENDS BOOK COVER

Add bits of thread or floss to the pulp after it has been pulsed. Stir them in with a spoon so that you don't damage the blender blades.

YOU WILL NEED

- blended pulp made from white lightweight paper, cream newsprint, purple mediumweight paper, and short lengths of embroidery floss

- cast-off book

- screen

- tissue paper

- deckle

- white craft glue

① Pour the blended pulp on the screen and remove the deckle.

② Allow the pulp to dry.

③ Break the dried paper into strips with irregular edges.

④ Noting overlaps, arrange the tissue paper and paper strips and attach them to the book cover with the white craft glue.

LOOK IT UP BOOK COVER

Paper pulp mixed with an old copy of the Yellow Pages makes for an interesting stew. This project is a great way to use up your pulpy leftovers.

YOU WILL NEED

- paper pulp made from white lightweight paper, cream newsprint, and pink mediumweight paper.

- shredded yellow pages

- papier-mâché paste (recipe on page 153)

- chunky book

- wax paper

- white craft glue

- rolling pin

① Place a sheet of wax paper on the craft table. Drop spoonfuls of paste on the paper.

② Arrange the shredded paper over the paste on the sheet of wax paper.

③ Add clumps of paper pulp.

④ Place a sheet of wax paper over the top and roll to compress.

⑤ Remove the wax paper and allow the compressed paper to dry.

⑥ Break an irregular shape from the dried paper and attach it to the book cover with the white craft glue.

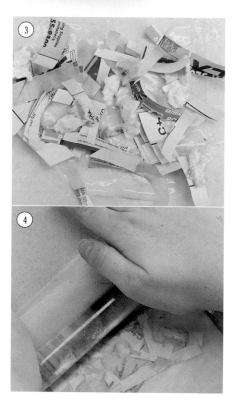

WINDOW BOX BACKDROP

Paper pulp mixed with rose petals and leaves makes for a day dreamy backdrop. Stir them into the pulp after it has been pulsed.

YOU WILL NEED

- blended pulp made from white lightweight paper, cream newsprint, pink mediumweight paper, and chopped petals and leaves
- window box frame
- 3-D accent
- white craft glue
- screen
- deckle

① Pour the blended pulp on the screen and remove the deckle.

② Allow the pulp to dry.

③ Break the dried paper into a rectangle with irregular edges.

④ Glue the paper to the back of the window box frame with white craft glue.

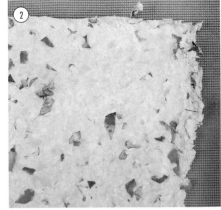

PAPER POT OF GOLD

A clay pot works as a terrific
molding form.

YOU WILL NEED

- blended pulp made from
  white lightweight paper, white
  mediumweight paper, and
  yellow mediumweight paper

- nonstick cooking spray

- clay pot

- decorative accents

- white craft glue

① Spray the clay pot with the nonstick
cooking spray. Shape the pulp over the
treated pot. Allow to dry.

② Remove the shaped paper pot from
the clay pot.

③ Attach the decorative accents to the
pot with the white craft glue.

Molded Paper

Molded paper combines softened pulp with white craft glue.
The dried paper is extra hard and extra durable.

YOU WILL NEED

- newspaper
- pot
- water
- bowl
- white craft glue
- wax paper

1. Tear or cut newspaper into small sections. Place them in a pot.

2. Cover the paper with hot water and let it sit overnight.

3. Transfer the mixture to a bowl.

4. Pour the water from the mixture. Knead the paper in the bowl to squeeze more water from the mixture.

5. Add 2 to 3 tablespoons of white craft glue to the mixture and work it into the pulp. Keep adding glue until the pulp sticks together.

6. Mold the mixture into the desired shapes with your hands. Place the shapes on wax paper to dry thoroughly. Store any leftover mixture in an airtight container.

To make beads or ornaments from the molded shapes, bore a shallow hole in the top with a needle.

Make a short wire loop and insert the ends in the hole. Apply a small drop of glue or varnish to secure.

Molded Paper Projects

MOLDED ACORNS

These craggy dried acorns mimic the appearance of those fashioned by Mother Nature. Only a real squirrel knows for sure.

YOU WILL NEED

- dough for molded paper
- wax paper
- acrylic paint
- flat modeling tool such as a knife or craft stick
- paintbrush

① Roll a clump of dough into a ball. Use the modeling tool to shape it into an acorn.

② Place it on wax paper to dry. Note that the acorn will shrink slightly when drying.

③ Paint as desired.

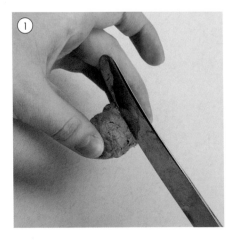

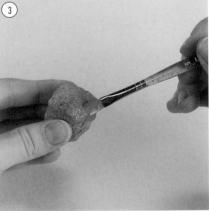

EGGS

There's no such thing as a rotten paper egg. Display these eggs for years to come.

YOU WILL NEED

• dough for molded paper

• wax paper

• acrylic paint

• paint brush

① Roll a clump of dough into a ball.

② Place it on wax paper to dry. Note that the egg will shrink slightly when drying.

③ Paint as desired.

MOLDED BEADS

Make beads in a variety of colors and sizes, and string them together for one-of-a-kind jewelry.

YOU WILL NEED

• dough for molded paper

• wax paper

• acrylic paint

• paintbrush

① Roll a clump of dough into a ball.

② Place it on wax paper to dry. Note that the bead will shrink slightly when drying.

③ Paint as desired.

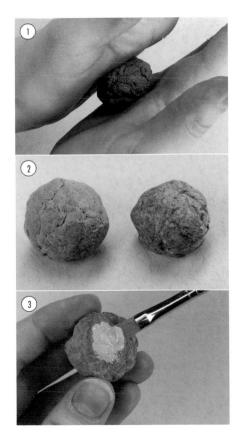

Templates

To copy the templates, layer tracing paper or sheer vellum over the selected shape. Carefully trace around the outline and cut along the marked line. Enlarge templates on a copy machine as indicated.

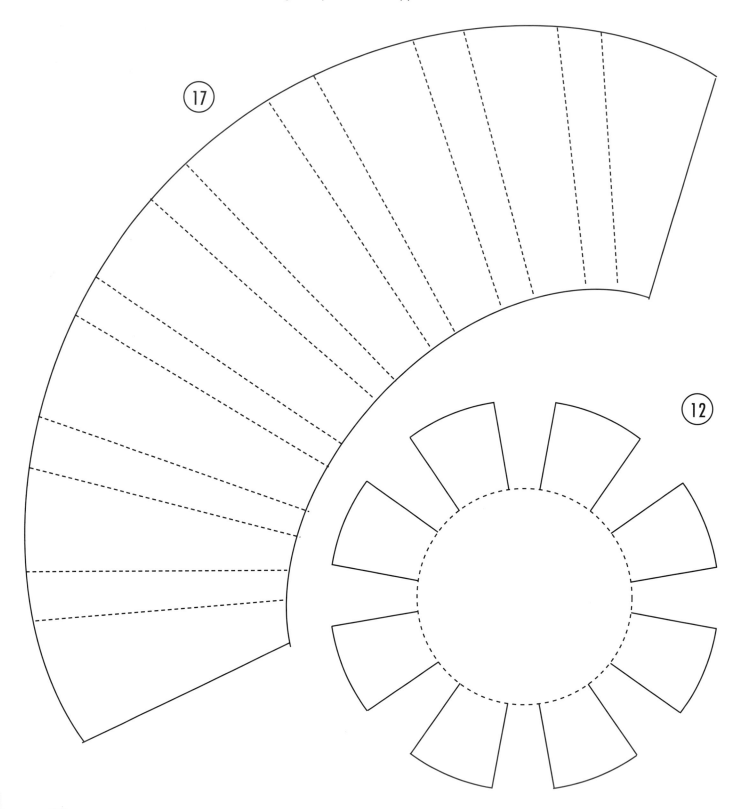

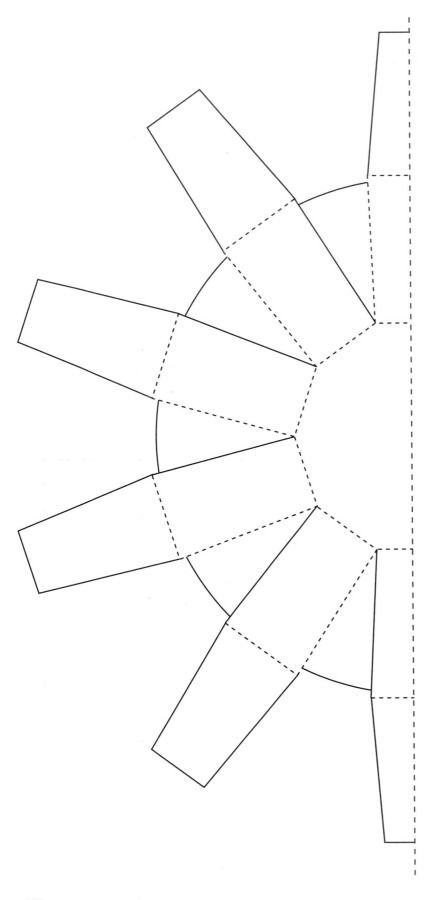

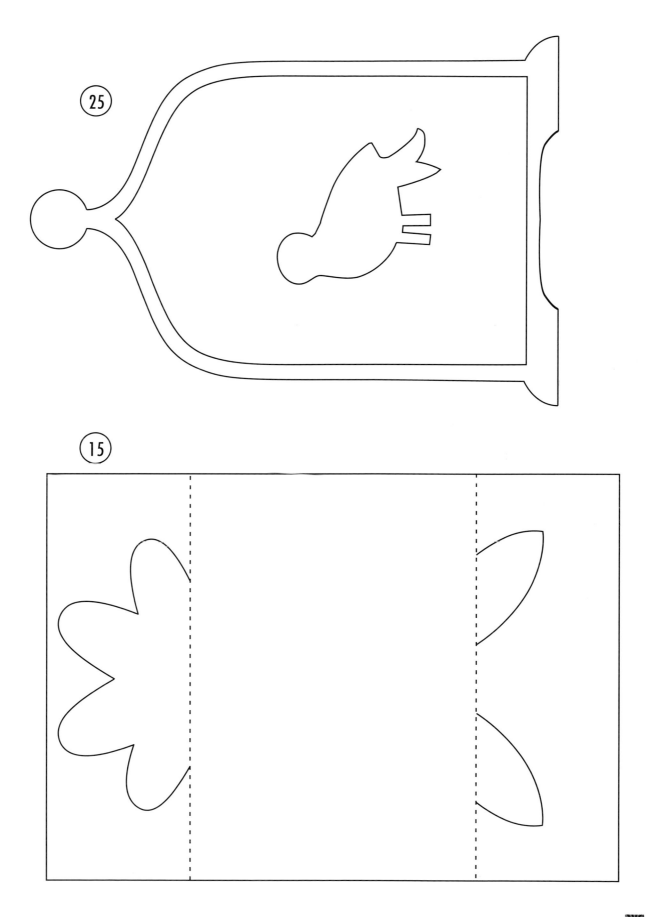

THE COMPLETE PHOTO GUIDE TO PAPER CRAFTS

Baby

33

Copy at 200%.

34

Copy at 200%.

THE COMPLETE PHOTO GUIDE TO PAPER CRAFTS

35

Copy at 200%.

36

Copy at 200%.

40

40

42

43

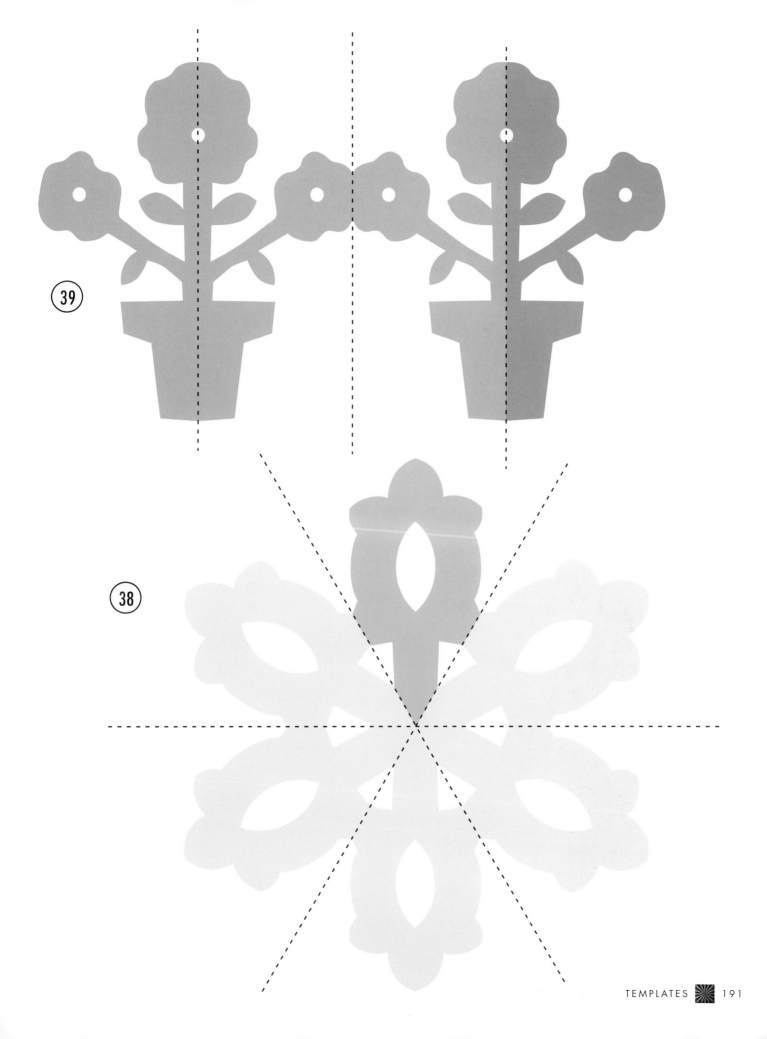

39

38

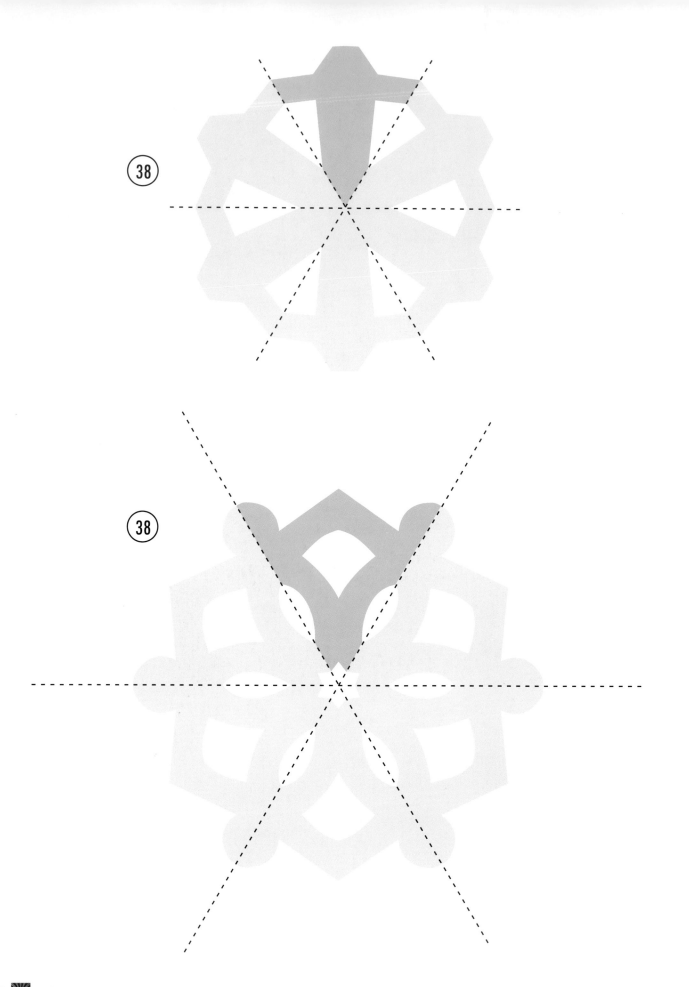

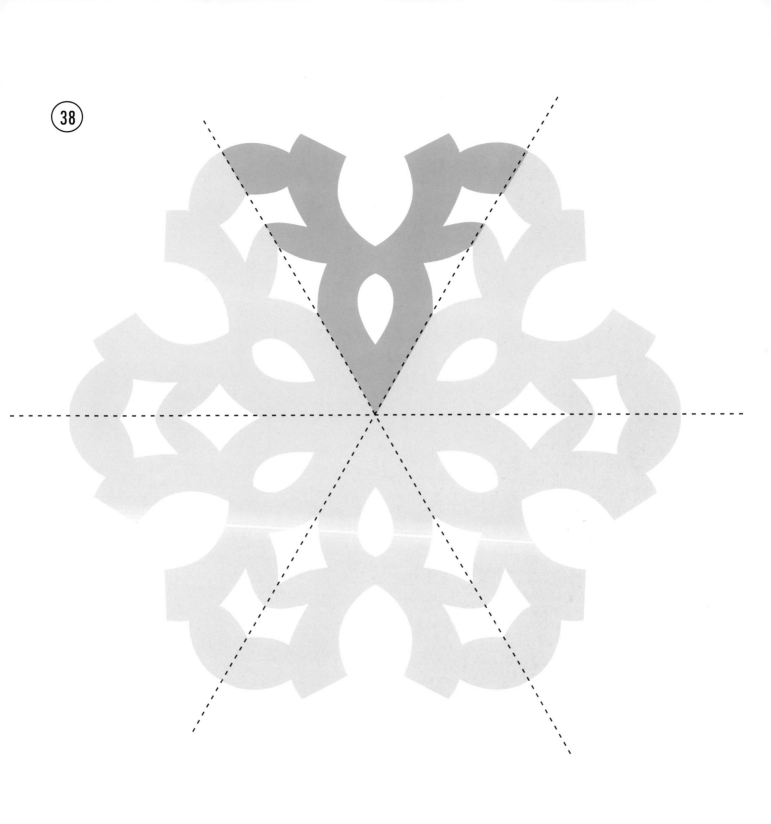

THE COMPLETE PHOTO GUIDE TO PAPER CRAFTS

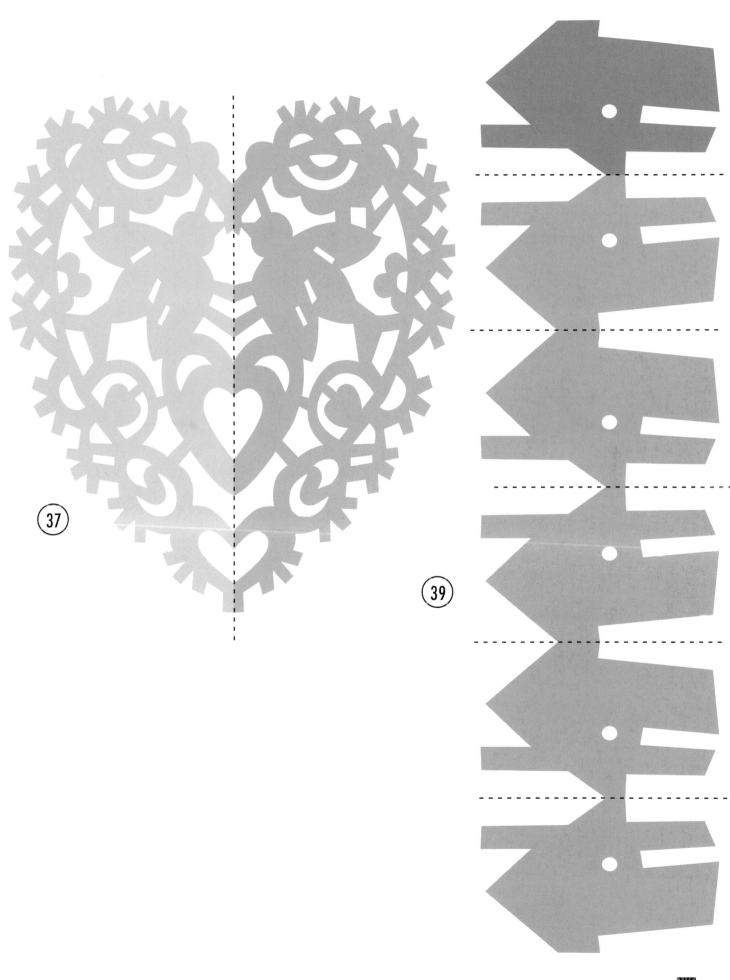

(37)

(39)

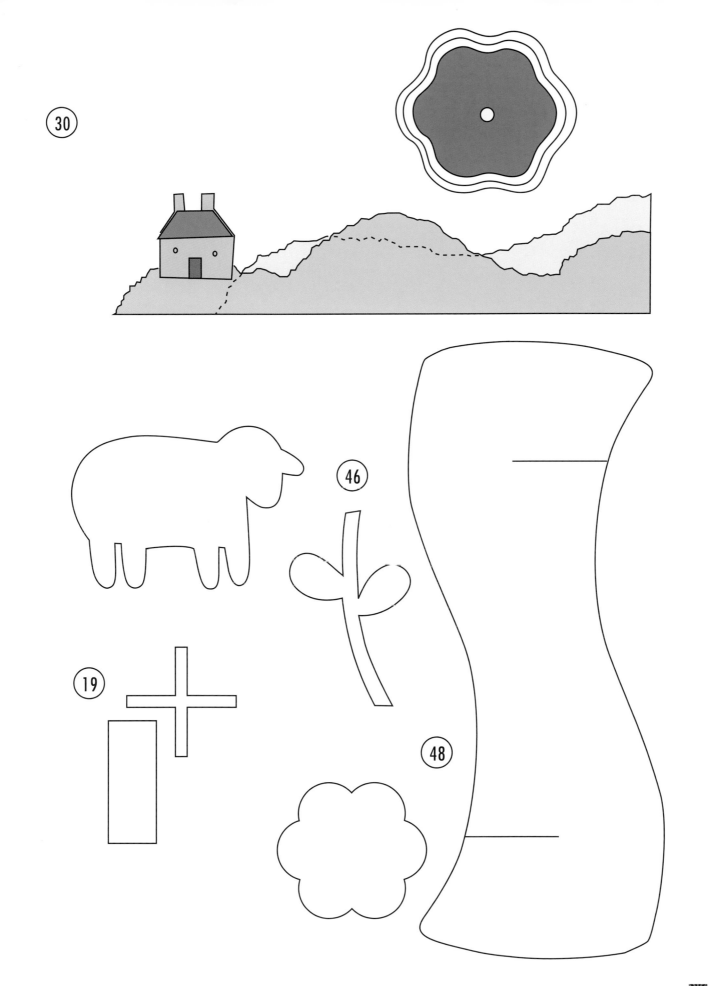

30

46

19

48

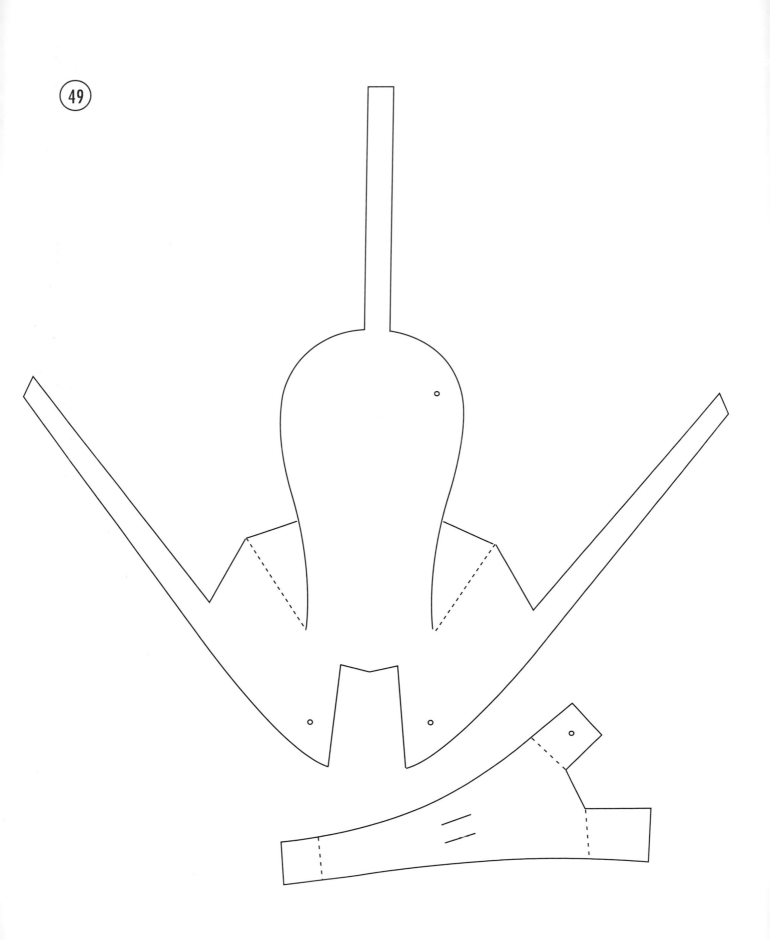

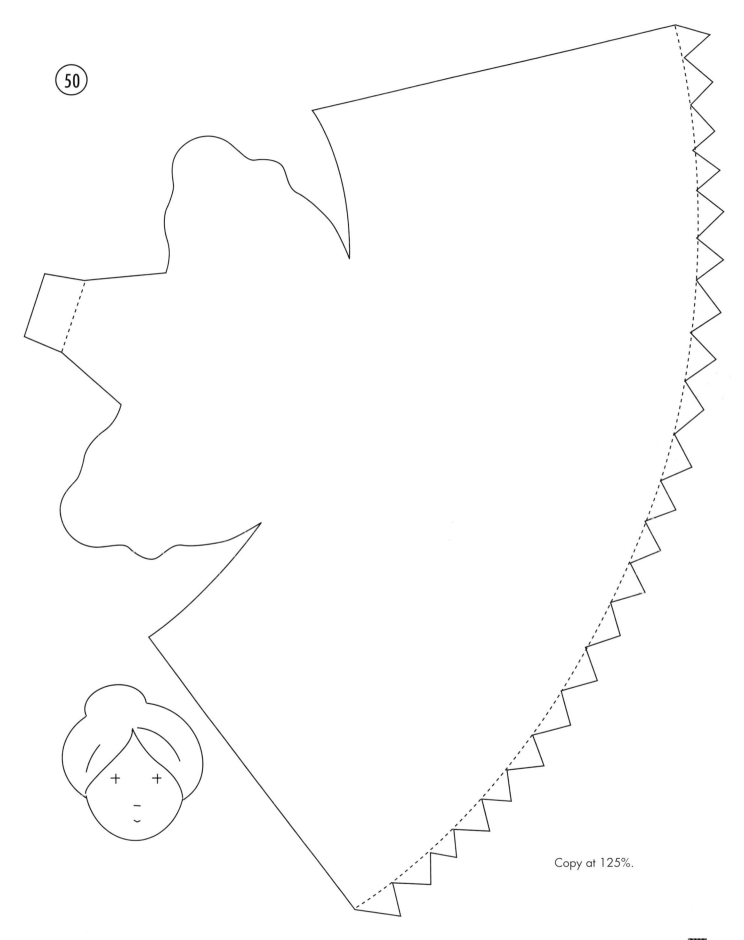

50

Copy at 125%.

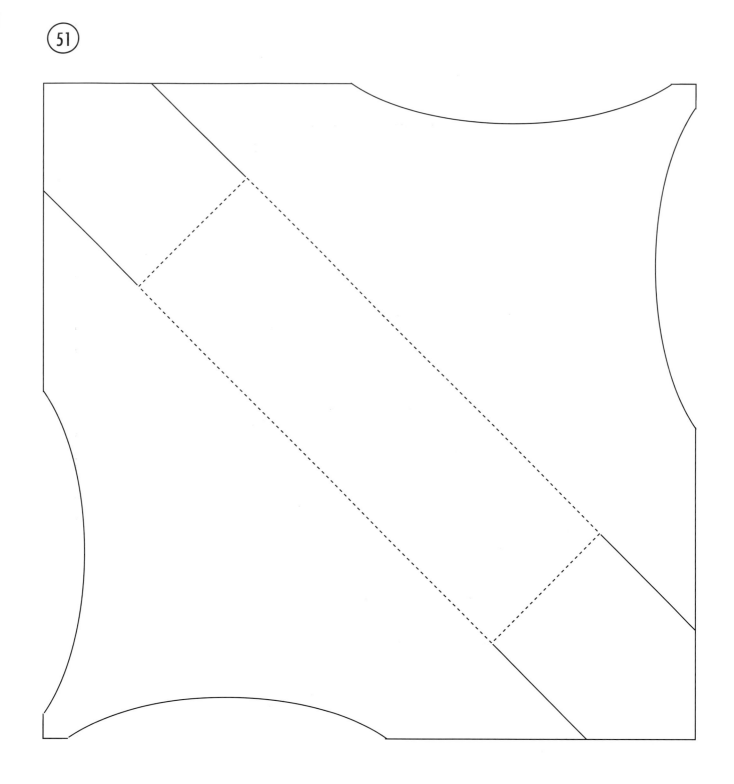

Copy at 125%.

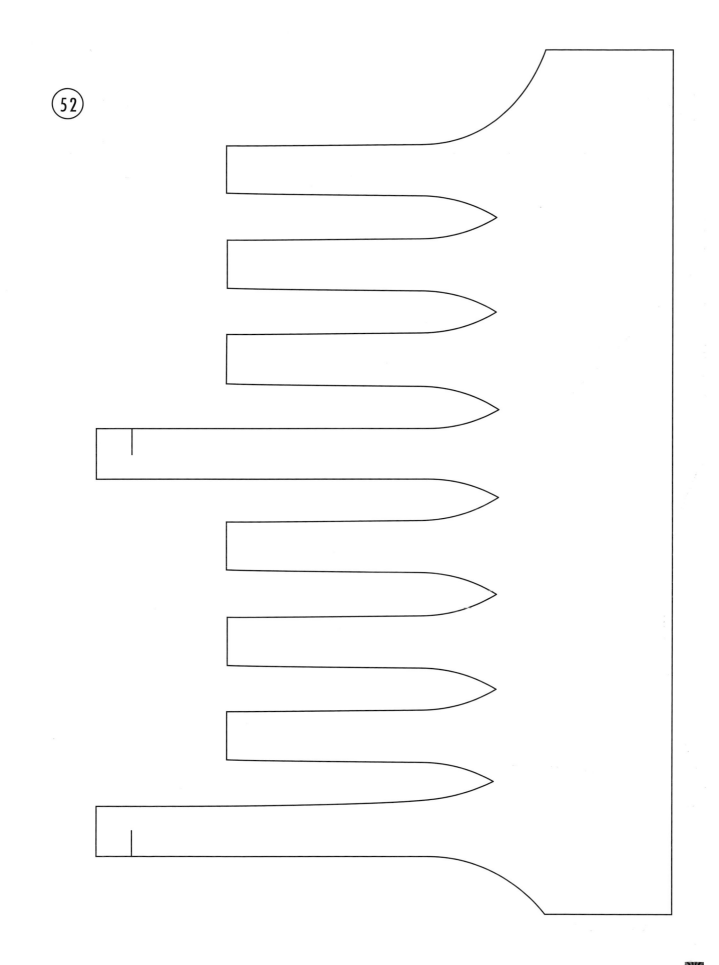

(52)

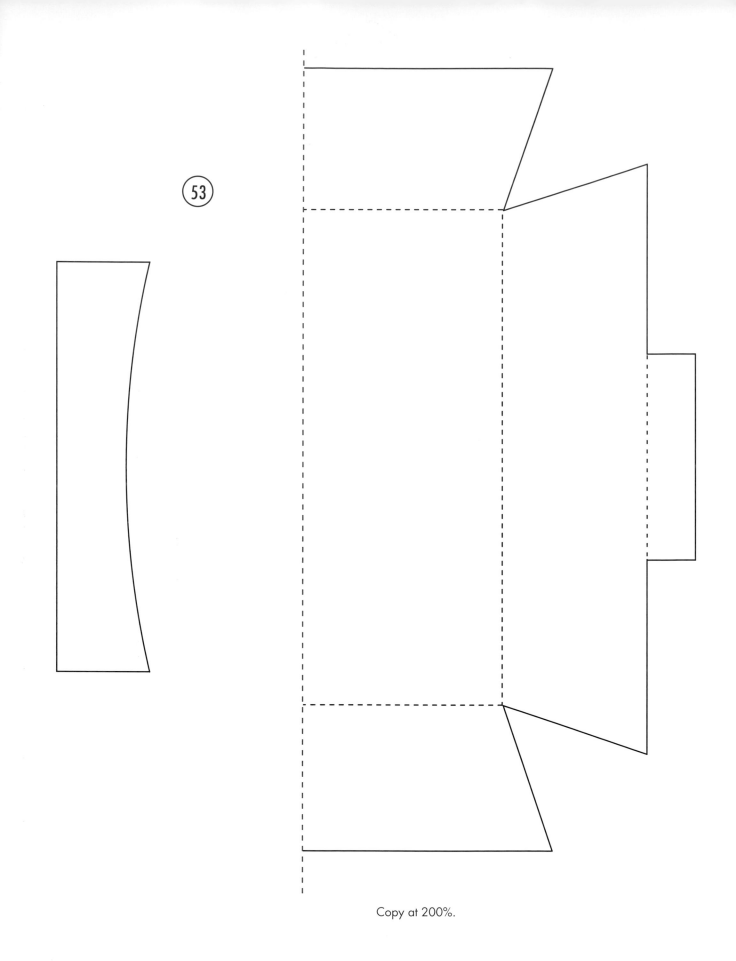

53

Copy at 200%.

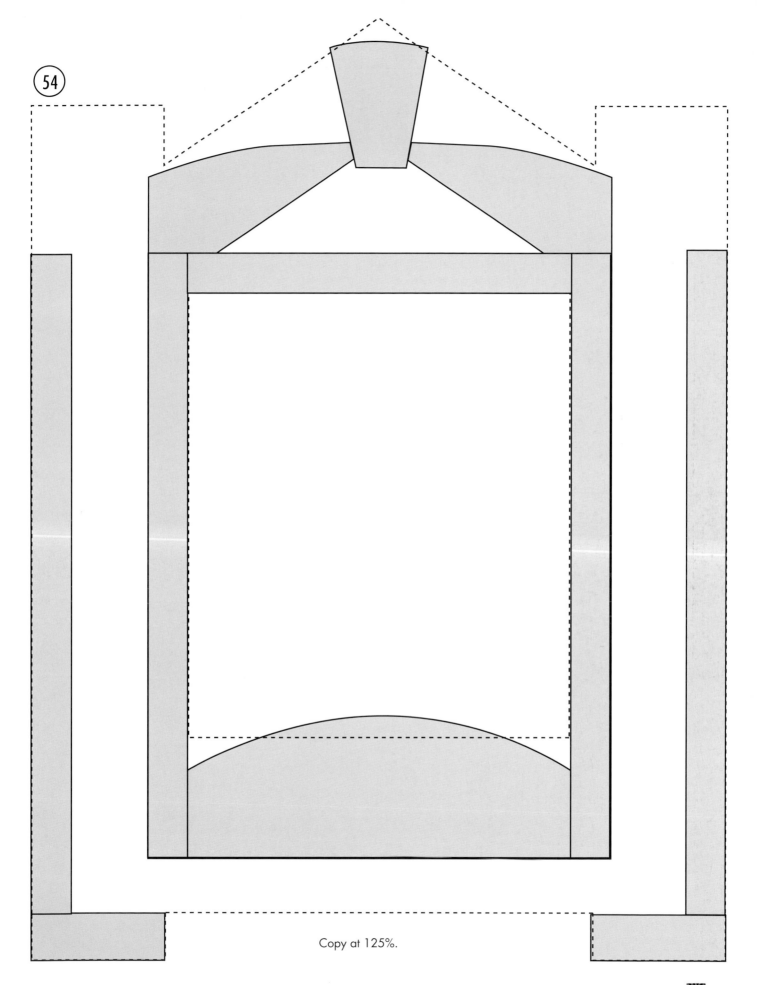

Copy at 125%.

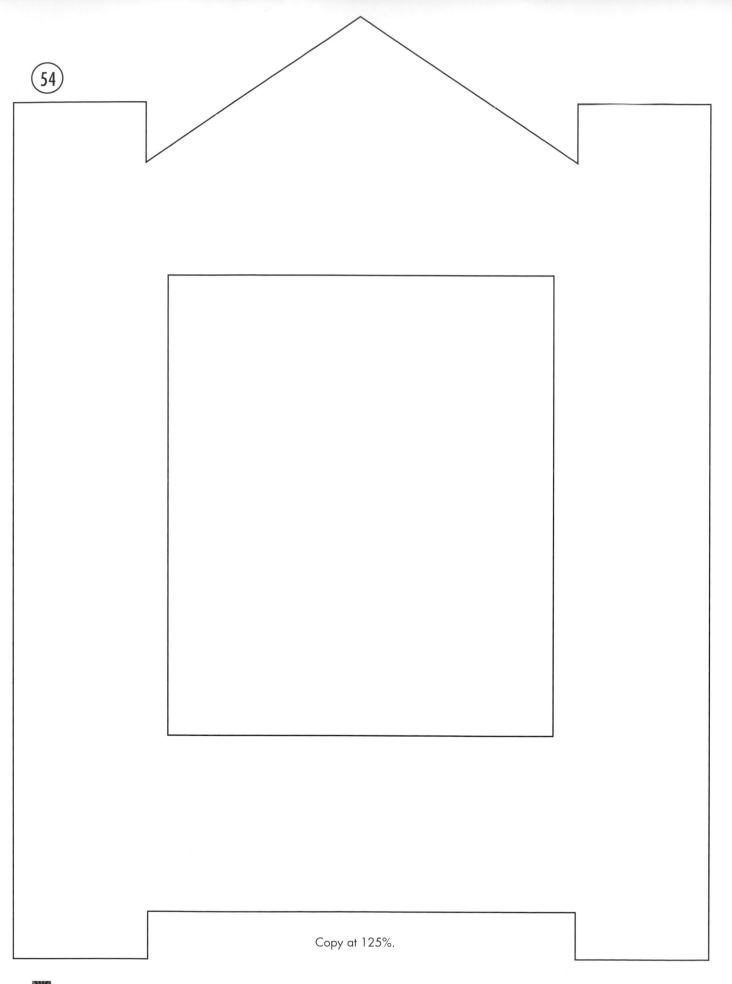

Copy at 125%.

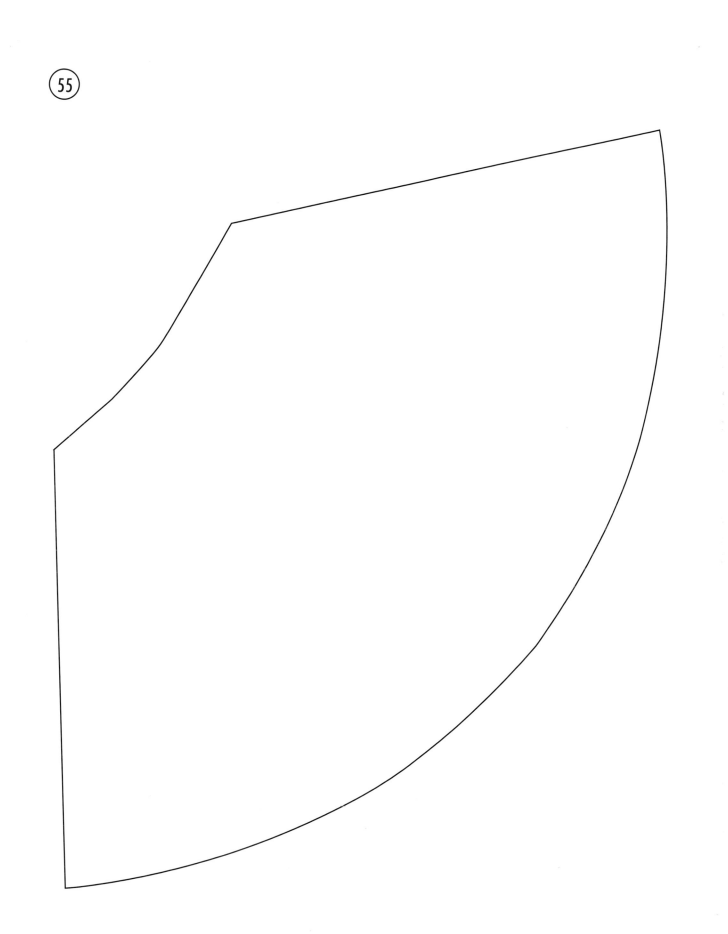

Index